KOREAN COOKBOOK

A twist on the traditional

Chung Jae Lee

KOREAN
COOKBOOK

twist on the traditional

NEW
HOLLAND

Chung Jae Lee

First published 2013 by
New Holland Publishers Pty Ltd
London · Cape Town · Sydney · Auckland

Garfield House 86–88 Edgware Road London W2 2EA United Kingdom
Wembley Square First Floor Solan Road Gardens Cape Town 8001 South Africa
1/66 Gibbes Street Chatswood NSW 2067 Australia
218 Lake Road Northcote Auckland New Zealand

www.newhollandpublishers.com

A record of this book is held at the British Library and National Library of Australia

ISBN 9781742573359

Publisher: Patsy Rowe
Designer: Keisha Galbraith
Editor: Jodi De Vantier
Photographs: Jacqui Way
Food stylist: Jacqui Way except pages 48, 63, 64, 74, 77, 81, 89 and 182 by Fiona Roberts.
Production director: Olga Dementiev
Printer: Toppan Leefung Printing Limited (China)

10 9 8 7 6 5 4 3 2 1

Keep up with New Holland Publishers on Facebook
www.facebook.com/NewHollandPublishers

Contents

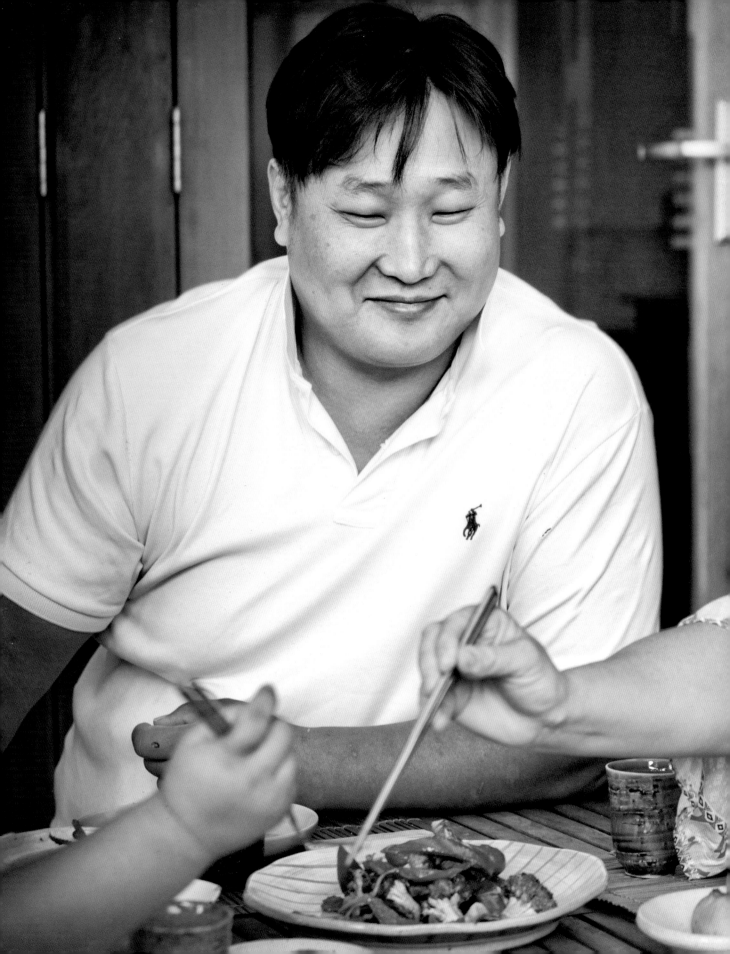

Introduction

I was born in the busy city of Seoul many moons ago now and food has always been and always will be a huge part of my life. Koreans love to eat and food must be delicious.

My mum and dad have always had businesses associated with food, giving anything a go—restaurants, bars and greengrocers—so the downside to them giving anything a go meant I didn't get to see them much when I was growing up. But it was easy to get a feed whenever I wanted, not just from my mum but also from our friendly customers. Korean people are very generous when it comes to food and as I would wander from table to table at the ripe old age of 4, I would get tastes from throughout the restaurant. My mother now tells me I would give 'puppy dog' eyes to the customers and walk up to their tables staring at them so they had to offer me some of their meal.

Mum and Dad worked hard seven days a week, at lunch and dinner, and had various different restaurants over my junior years. Our house was on the top level and the restaurant downstairs. My elder brother and sister and I would play upstairs in our house while mum and dad were busy downstairs in the restaurant. In Korea, every restaurant has one distinctive dish and in some cases some restaurants only sell this one dish accompanied with many sidedishes.

Being a 'larger lad' than most Koreans meant that I had a healthy appetite, so I would easily find my way into the restaurant numerous times during the day and night to enjoy my mum's delicious food. Mum has always been an inspiration to me with her talent to whip up something in the kitchen extremely fast—something that is healthy and delicious and looking so fresh when it is dished up.

In Korea and like many other Asian houses it is customary to take your shoes off before entering inside. The reasoning behind this is that the living area is where most families would eat and sleep. For example in our house when I was growing up we didn't have a dining table but a small fold-out table that we would bring out for each meal and sit on the floor while eating. Then at bedtime Mum would pull out the bed linen, place it over the floor where we had eaten dinner that day and that is where we would sleep—all five of us. So of course who would want dirty shoes trudged all over the floor where we eat and sleep?

We had a rooftop garden, which is where dad would grow a lot of fruit and vegetables in pots. This is where he would escape and enjoy the tranquillity of gardening. Chillies are a staple part in all Koreans' diet and my mum and dad would dry them and then make them into a chilli powder. In winter the rooftop would snow over, so drying whatever Dad could was how we would still enjoy home-grown produce in winter.

Most Korean households now own a kimchi fridge where an excess amount of kimchi that is made in summer can then be stored to eat in winter. Years ago the kimchi would be stored in large clay pots buried underground, and a lot of people still do this today as we can't live without kimchi. This is what you would do if you lived in country South Korea, as living in these areas is still very traditional. Kimchi is packed full of vitamins and the Koreans swear this is why the horrid SARS virus didn't make it into Korea years ago—because of their strong immune system from kimchi.

Growing up in Seoul may have been harder than other places, but I think my culture is a beautiful one and I have now picked the best out of it and combined it with my way of life here. In Seoul we have four distinctive seasons and various foods that we love to eat in these unique seasons. In summer we eat a lot of cold noodles, in autumn a lot of fruit, winter, of course, a lot of soups and in spring fresh micro herbs, sprouts and whatever is fresh from the ground. One of my favourite styles of eating is the barbecue. In fact, the district where I was born and grew up, the Mapo district, is where the Korean barbecue originated. People would light fires in 44-gallon drums, burning charcoal and cooking meats while sipping on soju, rice wine—some call it Korean rocket fuel. Mapo used to be a port when it was formed in 1944 but now consists of about 55 per cent residents, mainly in high-rise apartments, the rest of the land consists of green land including the World Cup Stadium and parklands along the famous Han River.

As in all Asian countries, eating on the streets is a must. It is delicious and inexpensive and sometimes this is dinner as office workers finish very late and start very early. The main street foods are dakgochi, dopoki, sundae, odang, orginjo teakim, mandu and hot dock. These are clean foods to have on the streets and also, depending on the seasons, you may get warm chestnuts, speckled corn on the cob or sweet potato chips. Also a popular and the best way to buy Yakult (10 cents) or Yoplait is from the ladies wheeling their carts around the streets—this is their livelihood and if you do your maths you'll see that's a lot to sell.

School lunches in Korea are quite different to other school lunches—definitely no sandwiches. My mum would make my lunch in a stainless steel lunch box and when we would get to school there would be a huge area where we would place ours over charcoal so it would continue to stay warm until the lunch bell rang. My lunch box usually consisted of rice, seaweed, kimchi and a meat of some sort. In grade 7 it changed and we didn't need to take lunch with us, just our own set of chopsticks and a spoon as the school supplied lunch.

School begins at the age of seven in Korea and starts around 8 AM but finishes at 12.30 PM and usually there are about 40 students in each class. There is a huge amount of pressure put on Korean children to do well at school and university so parents pay a fortune for private tutors. I guess that is why I developed my love for Martial Arts as it was definitely more fun. By the age of 10 I had my first black belt in tae kwon do

and then decided to try judo. The teachers got away with a lot then, like hitting us with sticks and making us try to kick down trees with our bare feet. In Korean society there is a huge emphasis on respecting your elders, which I am a true believer in, but in the school grounds the rules were a little tedious. I believe it was the dedication I learnt at Judo that has given me the dedication I have as a chef today.

I competed all through Korea and Japan and proved myself, and I know it must have been extremely tough on Mum and Dad but they were very supportive of me.

In South Korea it is compulsory for the males to attend the army for two and a half years, but I escaped that as I was deemed to be too expensive to join with my 'strong' physique—I think they were worried their food bill may have jumped up.

So after watching many documentaries and advertising, I decided to emigrate. I soon found my feet and can remember the smell of hot cross buns, which at first I didn't like but I now enjoy a well-made bun. That smell was one of my first impressions of my new home, and is something I won't ever forget.

I eventually settled in Adelaide as I knew there were not many Koreans living in this city so I would be forced to mix with more English speakers to improve my language skills. I continued my English studies here and when I had mastered it I commenced my next journey in life and studied to become a pilot for two years.

So as the story goes on I met Sam, a little country girl. So being a naïve Korean lad I didn't know she fancied me until her friend set us up and now we are married with two beautiful girls. Another huge life changing experience. We married in 2002 and then years later, in 2007, my sister and mum organised a wedding for us in Seoul.

I graduated as a pilot but as the world was in turmoil with September 11 I thought my chances of becoming a pilot were pretty slim so I suggested to Sam that we open a restaurant. With our love of dining out for good food and wine we soon learnt what to do and what not to do.

We started off with a small 30-seater place in a little laneway where we learnt the basics of restaurant life. My mum and sister came for a few months to help us set it up. It was an eye-opener for us all and we knew our new life was going to be tough. After 18 months, a restaurant became vacant in Gouger Street, the main eating hub of Adelaide—we decided to get it as there had been a fire in this location. And in Korean culture this means good luck for a business venture so I knew we had chosen the right location.

At the time of relocating to the larger restaurant in 2002 there were only a few Korean businesses around so we knew we had a hard slog ahead of us to introduce Korean cuisine and Korean culture to the locals. So I went ahead with a lot of advice from mum and a lot of experimenting on my friends and created a unique form of Korean cuisine.

I installed Korean TV and continued to eat out to expand my knowledge of the fast-growing food culture around me. Korean is fast becoming a new trend and a healthy option when eating Asian cuisine.

Introduction

Getting the new restaurant going wasn't easy—there were plenty of ups and downs making sure the prices were right and finding good suppliers. It was a harder slog than in the bigger cities but we have developed some loyal customers over the years. Just getting chefs was really difficult at first as no-one knew anything about Korean cuisine and it was hard to find Korean chefs. But my type of food developed with my own twist—I put love into every dish I make and I finish it off with my style of decoration too.

In 2009, I was lucky enough to be invited to attend a food conference in Jeju Island, South Korea as a presenter. I was one of three presenters to speak about how to showcase and make Korean food popular internationally. The other speakers were fellow Korean nationals living in China and the United States, who also had their own restaurants. This was a huge experience and I learnt a lot from the other speakers on how to market my own brand.

I remember when we first opened our new restaurant—Mapo—we had a very basic wine list with only mainstream wines that were available from every bottle shop around, but that has certainly changed too as we started focusing on local wines matched to the food we served. In 2012 this paid off as we were a finalist in the *Gourmet Traveller* Wine List Awards, getting us a glass mark which makes us the first Korean restaurant to achieve this in Australia. We now have a huge number of local winemakers support us and dine in regularly, sometimes doing wine dinners and wine pairing with various degustation menus.

Mapo has racked up some accolades over the years, the most recent being the 2012 State Champion for 'Flavours of the World' Lifestyle Food. We were awarded a Good Food Guide Chef Hat in 2012, and awarded Best Asian in 2010 and 2011 at the Restaurant and Catering 'Awards for Excellence', making us National Finalists. In all of these awards we have been the first Korean restaurant to achieve these prestigious accolades.

I am ecstatic with my latest award, SA 'Chef of the Year', which I received at the 2012 Awards for Excellence. This is a huge feather in my cap and I am the only Korean ever to get this award, so any of you out there too scared to try, just do it as you never know what this may lead to—the sky is the limit.

With a good upbringing and supportive parents and wife, I have developed a strong desire and goal to become a successful and renowned chef, taking Korean cuisine to another level here and around the world. It has been tough not having my family around me but who knows what may happen. I think Seoul may also need a Mapo restaurant in the near future.

Chung Jae Lee

Table manners in Korea

As a young boy growing up in Seoul we had rules to follow when eating—rules that required patience. As I was a 'strong' little man with a healthy appetite it was hard for me to resist the temptation of just delving into the food headfirst. I think these rules are fairly much the same as Western table manners.

These simple rules, followed in all Korean households, are:
- ⊙ The older members at the table must start eating first, then you can follow in 'rank'.
- ⊙ Try to keep up with the older members while eating.
- ⊙ Do not hold the spoon and chopsticks together in one hand at the same time.
- ⊙ At the end of your meal try not to put your chopsticks and spoon down first; wait for the older people at the table.
- ⊙ Don't reach too far across the table to get the food you desire.

A child's first birthday (Tol)

The celebration of a child's first birthday in Korea is huge, and quite often a hall is hired for the ceremony (party) because the houses are too small for the number of guests invited.

The parents prepare a special Tol table with a variety of over 12 ddeok (rice cakes) and seasonal fruit.

The Tol is also a ceremony where the child decides his/her destiny in life by choosing an item laid out in front of them that has a significant meaning. On the table the parents place:

Thread/Wool:	the child will live long
Jujube:	the child will have many descendants
Book, pencil, ruler:	the child will become a successful scholar
Paintbrush:	the child will be artistic
Rice:	the child will become rich
Needle, scissors:	the child will be talented with his/her hands
Knife:	the child will be a good cook

The birthday child will go around the table and pick up items that he/she is attracted to, and the child's future is predicted according to what is grabbed. A traditional screen is often used behind the child to assist with photographs.

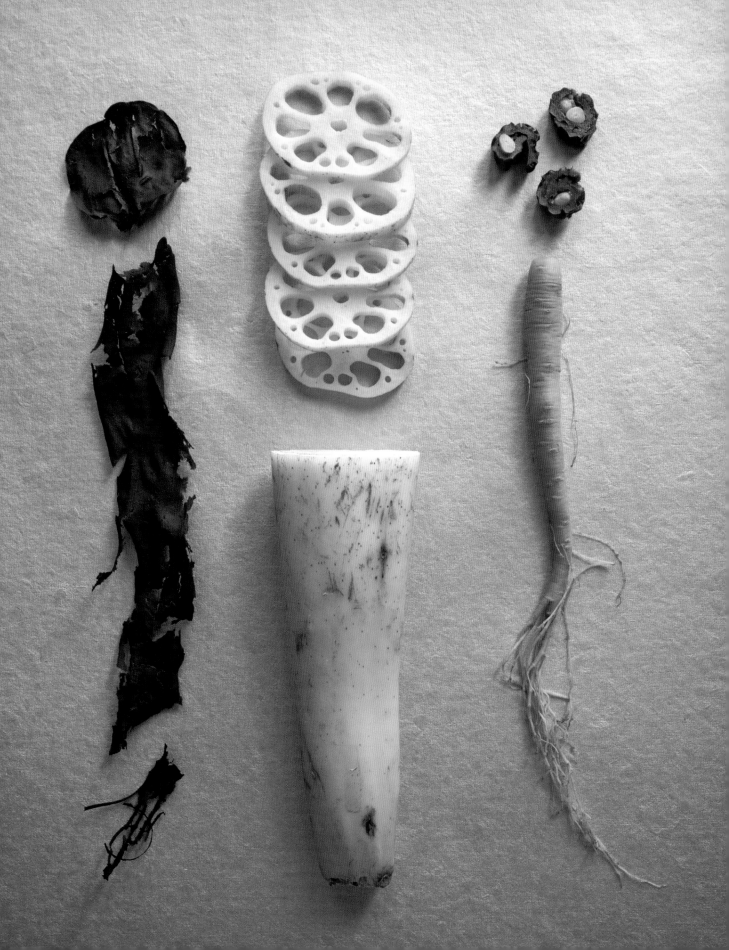

Necessities for your Korean kitchen

Korean beef stock (dashida)
: This is an exotic powdered seasoning made from shank broth. Great for soups and stews.

Korean chilli paste (gochujang)
: This was traditionally made in large outdoor pots and left to ferment over the years. Made by combining red peppers, glutinous rice, and soy bean paste and left to mature in the sun.

Korean chilli powder (gochu gadu)
: Made from dried red peppers. Simply made by cutting off the stems of fresh chillies and removing the seeds, then opened up and left to dry in the sun for a couple of weeks. The dried chillies are then ground up until you have a fine powder.

Garlic

Ginger

Korean or Japanese soy sauce
: Both kinds of soy sauce is made from fermented beans. The word for soy sauce in Korean, means 'salty'

Sugar syrup

Soju or sake
: Soju is Korean rice wine, a clear, vodka-like beverage popular with Koreans. It can range from 17%–45% in alcohol volume.

Potato starch

Doenjang
: Soy bean paste made from fermented solid ingredients of soy sauce.

Fish sauce

Sesame oil

Sesame seeds

Tempura powder

Seaweed
: There are a number of varieties, all classed as a health food, as it is rich in minerals.

potato
starch

soju

fish
sauce

sugar
syrup

sesame
seeds

soy
sauce

chilli
powder

seaweed

chilli paste

beef stock

ginger

doenjang

sesame
oil

garlic

tempura
powder

Asian-style cuts of beef

Chuck: Good for bulgogi, steak or pan-frying.

Tenderloin: This is an expensive cut of steak.

Sirloin strip: Also good for bulgogi.

Prime ribs: This is very popular for Koreans and is full of flavour. Good for barbecuing, pan-frying or slow cooking.

Rump: There is a lot of muscle in this cut so it needs to be marinated. Coca-Cola is a good marinade for this.

Brisket: Great for soups or slow cooking. Always used in jigaes. Jigae is similar in texture to a stew and has many varieties, typically made with meat or seafood.

party food

Tempura Oysters with Grilled Shrimp

Serves 2–4

Mapo customers love tempura oysters so I thought I would add to this dish by introducing something extra.

1 egg yolk
500ml (17½fl oz) cold water
Oil for deep-frying
¼ cup tempura powder (available from supermarkets or Asian grocery stores)
12 fresh oysters
8 prawns (shrimp)
Salt
Pepper
2 eggs
¼ apple
8 chives
Tartare Sauce (see recipe)
Sesame oil

Preheat the oven to 180°C (350°F). Whisk the egg yolk and water together and put in the fridge to chill, as the colder the batter the crunchier it will be once fried.

In a wok or large frypan, heat the oil on a slow heat for about 15 minutes. To test it is hot enough, sprinkle on a little salt and if it sizzles you know it's ready.

Add the tempura powder to the egg yolk and water, whisking together to form a paste, which becomes tempura batter. Add the oyster meat to the paste ensuring to coat well. Now put the meat in the hot oil and they should be cooked in 3–4 minutes. You will know when they are ready as the oysters will float to the top and then to the side, turning a lovely golden brown.

Peel the shells off the prawns, leaving the heads and tails. Score the back with a knife and devein. Spread the flesh flat out on a lined baking tray, put slits in the flesh and then season with salt and pepper.

Place the prawns in the oven for approximately 10 minutes or until cooked. While they are cooking, prepare the apple and chives.

Separate the eggs and whisk. Then in a frypan (small square shape preferable) lightly fry first the white and then the yolk in a small amount of oil. Then set aside to cool before cutting into lengths about 2 x .2cm (¾ x ⅛in). Wash and cut the apple and chives into lengths of 2cm (¾in).

To serve, put a teaspoon of tartare sauce in cleaned and dried oyster shells and put the tempura oyster meat in each one. Then on the same plate lay the prawns down and splash with a little sesame oil. Carefully place the egg white and egg yolk strips in small bundles, along with the apple and chives across the back of the prawns.

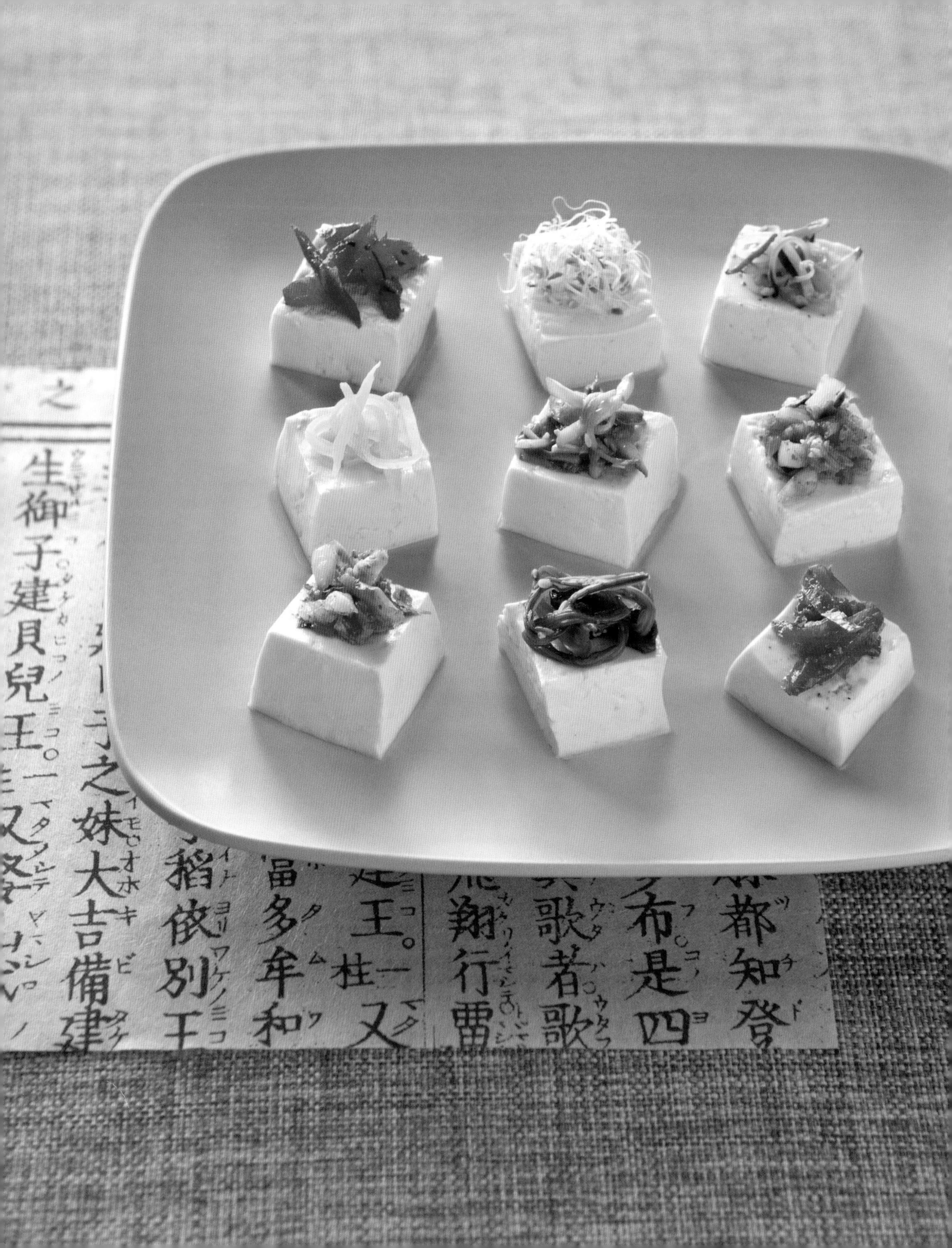

Tofu Canapé

Perfect with a nice glass of champagne at your next dinner party.

1 tablespoon oil
50g (1¾oz) Swiss brown
   mushrooms, finely sliced
1 teaspoon sugar
1 teaspoon Korean soy sauce
1 teaspoon minced garlic
½ tablespoon oil
Pinch sesame seeds
50g (1¾oz) zucchini (courgette),
   julienned
Pinch salt
Pinch pepper
1 teaspoon sesame oil
½ teaspoon sesame seeds

50g (1¾oz) pickled radish, sliced
   thinly
1 tablespoon vinegar
½ tablespoon sugar
3 tablespoons water

70g (2oz) kimchi
1 teaspoon sugar
1 teaspoon sesame oil
Pinch sesame seeds

50g (1¾oz) sundried tomatoes
50g (1¾oz) English spinach
1 tablespoon sesame oil
1 tablespoon minced garlic
Pinch salt
Pinch pepper
500g (17½oz) firm tofu

Preheat oven to 180°C (350°F).

Heat oil in a pan and fry mushrooms with sugar, soy sauce, minced garlic and sesame seeds until just soft. Set aside in a small bowl.

Heat the oil in a pan and fry the zucchini with salt, pepper, sesame oil and sesame seeds until soft, but don't overcook. Set aside in a small bowl.

Mix the radish gently with vinegar, sugar and water. Set aside.

Fry the kimchi with the sugar, sesame oil and sesame seeds for 3–4 minutes. Set aside in a small bowl.

Dice the sundried tomatoes into small pieces.

Wash and drain the English spinach and cut finely into 1cm (¼in) lengths. Then heat the sesame oil in a frypan and add the spinach, garlic, salt and pepper. This should only take about 2–3 minutes to cook.

Cut the tofu evenly into 12 pieces and, with a melon ball scoop, carefully remove a small amount of tofu where the vegetables will sit. Place tofu on a lined baking tray and sprinkle with salt and pepper. Then place the tofu in the oven for 10 minutes.

You will have enough topping to make two canapés of each style with the already prepared vegetables by simply styling the vegetables on top, creating an exquisite tofu canapé.

Periwinkles in Serrano Ham

Serves 2

These are a delicacy in Asian countries and are full of protein. My mum taught me how to cook them without being chewy and here they are ... delicious to eat anytime.

Water
10 periwinkles
1 tablespoon salt
1 tablespoon butter
1 tablespoon pepper
5 pieces serrano ham

In a large bowl, add enough cold water to cover the periwinkles and add the salt. Leave for about 2 hours to remove the sea salt. Then wash thoroughly and leave to drain.

In a saucepan add two cups of water and bring to the boil. When boiling, add the periwinkles and leave boiling for 5 minutes.

With a pin or toothpick remove the 'little lid' from the periwinkles and take out the meat. In a frypan, melt the butter, add the pepper and toss the periwinkle meat in, just long enough to coat it. Set aside.

Slice each piece of ham lengthways. Then either grill or slightly fry the ham until lightly crispy.

Carefully wrap the periwinkle in the ham and put each one back in its shell to serve.

Beef Wrapped in Fried Rice
Bulgogi Bokumbap Sum

This is simple yet very tasty. I love fried rice, especially when you mix it with beef.

MARINADE
1 tablespoon palm sugar
2 tablespoons Korean soy sauce
1 tablespoon sugar
1 tablespoon minced garlic
1 tablespoon white wine
½ teaspoon sesame seeds

8 thin sirloin strips
1 tablespoon oil
¼ onion, diced
½ carrot, diced
¼ red capsicum (bell pepper),
   diced
8 tiger prawns (shrimp), peeled
   and deveined
½ cup cooked, cold rice
Pinch salt
1 tablespoon oil

In a pot, melt the palm sugar and then turn off the heat and add the remaining marinade ingredients until well combined. Then marinate the sirloin for a minimum of one hour.

Heat the oil in a frypan and cook the onion, tossing quickly, then the carrot and capsicum. Add the washed prawns and toss gently until the prawns are cooked, then add the cooked rice and toss through, adding the salt to taste.

When the beef is ready, lay each piece out flat. Evenly divide the rice and prawn mix into eight.

Place the mix in the beef and roll with the prawn tail sticking out one end.

In a frypan heat the oil and fry on a low heat until cooked to your liking.

Street Food
Petite Kimbab

This is great for a kid's birthday party and obviously not full of sugar so the parents will love you. Also great as finger food for the adults.

3 cups water
Pinch salt
150g (5oz) English spinach

SPINACH MARINADE
⅓ teaspoon fish sauce
Pinch salt
Pinch sesame seed
½ tablespoon minced garlic

2 carrots
1 teaspoon oil
Pinch salt
3 bowls warm cooked rice (see
    Steamed Rice recipe)
½ tablespoon sesame seeds
2 tablespoons sesame oil
Pinch salt
6 sheets sushi seaweed
6 strips pickled yellow radish (the
    radish can be purchased in
    strips so just cut to the desired
    length)

KIMBAP SAUCE
½ tablespoon honey mustard
1 tablespoon Korean or Japanese
    soy sauce
½ tablespoon white vinegar
1 tablespoon sugar syrup
¼ tablespoon wasabi (optional)

In a saucepan, bring to the boil 3 cups water and add a pinch of salt. When boiling, add the spinach and blanch for approximately 3 minutes or until soft but still a bright green.

Remove and drain while washing thoroughly. The best way to remove the excess water is to squeeze it out by hand. Put in a mixing bowl and add the spinach marinade ingredients and toss together by hand.

Peel the carrots and cut julienne-style about 4cm (1½in) in length and ½cm (¼in) thick, then in a frypan add the oil and fry until soft with salt. Don't overcook as you want to keep the colour vibrant orange.

Add to the cooked rice the sesame seeds, sesame oil and pinch salt and when the rice is cooled you are ready to assemble the kimbap.

On a chopping board cut each seaweed sheet into quarters. Spread a thin layer of rice onto the seaweed leaving a 1cm (¼in) strip at the top of the square.

In the middle of the seaweed place a strip of the English spinach, radish and carrot mix. On the 1cm (¼in) strip at the top use your finger to brush some sesame oil to make the seaweed stick together. Now roll and press firmly to make sure it is sealed.

To make the kimbap sauce, mix all ingredients together and use as a dipping sauce. Not everyone likes wasabi so this is optional.

This can be served with toothpicks or on a plate. If you wish you can paint some extra sesame oil on top and sprinkle over some sesame seeds.

Korean-style Shrimp Cocktail

Serves 8

My mother-in-law introduced me to shrimp cocktails on Christmas Day. This is my version.

8 tiger prawns (shrimp)
Salt
Pepper
2 tablespoons oil
8 pieces white bread
Tartare Sauce (see recipe)
16 cucumber slices
8 iceberg lettuce leaves, washed
    and drained
8 mint leaves, washed and
    drained
100g (3½oz) fish roe (flying fish
    eggs)
Butter

Firstly, devein the prawns and wash well, drying with a towel to remove any excess water. Sprinkle a little salt and pepper on them. In a frypan heat some oil and pan-fry the prawns until cooked. Set aside to cool.

Remove the crusts and with a rolling pin flatten each piece of bread, then lightly spread the tartare sauce on each slice and add a prawn, 2 slices of cucumber, a lettuce leaf, a mint leaf and a teaspoon of fish roe. Spread out and roll the cocktail in the bread.

In a frypan on a low heat add a very small amount of butter and lightly fry your prawn cocktails until just toasted.

A great alternative for your Christmas Day lunch.

String Beans and Scallops

Fast, simple and tasty. Great for a snack or as a side.

8 string beans
½ zucchini (courgette)
½ red capsicum (bell pepper)
1 tablespoon butter
¼ cup fried onions
Salt
Pepper
2 tablespoons coconut milk
2 tablespoons Ginger-flavoured
  Sweet Soy Sauce (see recipe)
8 Japanese scallops
Oil for frying

Finely dice the string beans, zucchini and capsicum.

In a frypan on a high heat, add the butter, beans, zucchini and capsicum and fry until just soft. Then add the fried onions, salt and pepper, coconut milk and sweet soy sauce.

Pan-fry the scallops with a pinch of salt and pepper on each side in a little oil until golden brown.

To serve, place the bean mixture on top of each scallop and it is ready to eat.

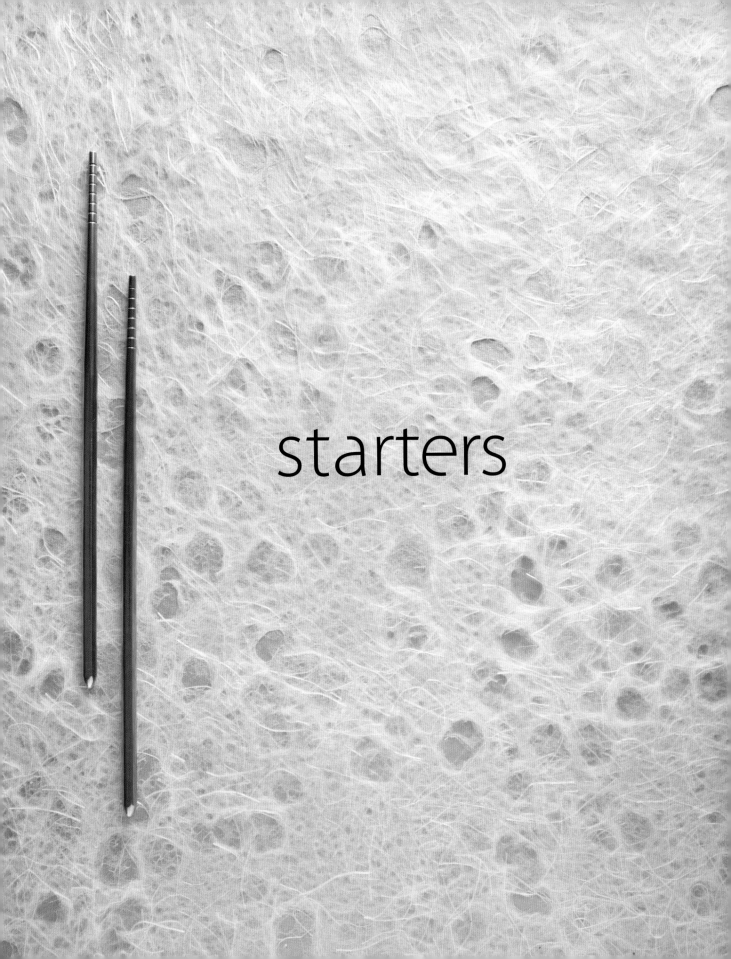

starters

Mushroom Wontons

Serves 4

This is my version of ravioli—a lot spicier and a great vegetarian option.

2 red onions, finely diced
3 bunches garlic chives, finely
  chopped
200g (7oz) shiitake mushrooms,
  finely diced
200g (7oz) Swiss brown
  mushrooms, finely diced
1 pkt (500g/17½oz) firm tofu
2 eggs
wonton wrappers
½ cup plain (all-purpose) flour

SAUCE
2 tablespoons oil
4 tablespoons Korean chilli
  powder
2 tablespoons minced garlic
1 tablespoon sugar
1 teaspoon salt
Pinch pepper
1 brown onion, finely chopped
4 birdseye chillies, finely sliced
½ cup Chinese cabbage, finely
  sliced
2 stems spring onion (scallion),
  finely sliced
20ml (⅔fl oz) water
1 saffron thread (optional)
Oil

Put the onion, chives, and both mushroom varieties in a mixing bowl. In a blender, put the tofu and eggs, blend until it becomes a smooth paste and then mix together with the vegetables.

To assemble the wontons, put one wonton wrapper in one hand and place one teaspoon of mixture in the middle. Carefully, with the other hand, dot water around the edge of the wrapper, then place a second wrapper on top of the other and press the edges down firmly so they are sealed.

On an already prepared tray sprinkled with the plain flour, place the wontons one by one as you make them.

To make the sauce, put the oil in a saucepan and when hot add the chilli powder and garlic. Reduce the heat and fry until the colour appears bright red. Add the sugar, salt, pepper, onion, chilli, cabbage, spring onion and water and boil for 30 minutes, then reduce the heat and simmer for 15 minutes. Add the saffron thread.

To cook the wontons, heat the oil in a large frypan on a medium heat and add the wontons in batches of 6 until they are browned on each side, then add 2 ladles of the sauce and simmer for 2 minutes. Then they are ready to serve.

Chicken Roll

Serves 4

In Asia, there are a lot of chicken dishes but they are mainly deep-fried. So I decided to create a healthy chicken dish and add in some vegetables.

2 chicken breasts
2 tablespoons white wine
Pinch salt
Pinch pepper
6 walnuts
4 tablespoons Spinach (see recipe in Sides chapter)
2 slices of your favourite cheese
1 teaspoon minced garlic
2 tablespoons butter
2 tablespoons oil
Walnut Sauce (see recipe)
2 tablespoons Korean chilli paste

Butterfly-cut the chicken breast and, using a meat tenderiser, lightly spread the meat out.

Marinate the chicken in the white wine, salt and pepper and leave in the fridge for 30 minutes.

Dice the walnuts, spinach and cheese and carefully place them lengthways in the middle of one side of the chicken. Add the garlic and butter and roll the breast. Make sure to press down firmly so the filling will not escape.

In a frypan, heat the oil and on a medium heat fry the chicken. Or, if you prefer, you can bake in the oven for 20 minutes at 220°C (430°F).

Carefully slice the chicken, which will resemble sushi pieces, and serve on a plate. Drizzle over with the walnut sauce on one side and the chilli paste on the other as they are both great dipping sauces.

Ginger Pork Balls

This is a favourite with young and old and also on the menu in my restaurant.

3 brown onions, finely diced
1kg (2lb 4oz) minced pork
1 tablespoon minced ginger
1 tablespoon minced garlic
100ml (3½fl oz) white wine or soju
  (Korean rice wine)
½ teaspoon pepper
2 tablespoons Korean beef stock
2 tablespoons sugar
3 tablespoons Korean soy sauce
1 egg
20g (²/₃oz) potato starch (potato
  flour)
Extra potato starch, for rolling
1 litre (44fl oz) cooking oil
1 cup tempura powder
3 cups iced water

Place the onions, pork mince, ginger and garlic in a mixing bowl and combine with your hands.

Now put the white wine, pepper, beef stock, sugar, soy sauce and egg in a blender and mix together to make a juice.

Add the juice and potato starch to the mince mixture and thoroughly mix with your hands for around 5 minutes, ensuring all is well combined. Set aside for 10 minutes.

Sprinkle enough potato starch for rolling on a tray and roll the mixture into balls the size of a golf ball. Roll in the starch on the tray.

In a large frypan or wok, heat the oil then reduce to medium heat, add the balls and when they float to the top they are cooked.

Drain on baking paper or in a colander.

In a bowl, add the tempura powder and roll in the cooked balls, coating them well. Now add the iced water to the remaining tempura powder, mixing well, and just before putting the balls back into the oil quickly dip in the tempura batter. Cook the balls again until they turn dark brown—they are now ready.

Seafood Money Bags

Serves 4

A very popular dish in my restaurant, Mapo.

200g (7oz) basa fillet
150g (5oz) squid
50g (1¾oz) prawns (shrimp),
    peeled, broken into pieces
½ cup fresh Thai basil
1 tablespoon lemon juice
2 brown onions, finely diced
1 teaspoon pepper
1 teaspoon salt
1 tablespoon sugar
5 tablespoons potato starch (corn
    flour)
1 litre (36fl oz) oil
20 stems garlic chives
2 pkt wonton wrappers (about 20)
Peanut Sauce (see recipe)
Tartare Sauce (see recipe)

Chop the basa, squid and prawns, put in a food processor and blend with the Thai basil and lemon juice until it is smooth.

Combine the onion with the seafood mix, stirring with a wooden spoon, and slowly add the pepper, salt, sugar and potato starch. Mix until well combined.

When all combined, cover with wrap, leave in the fridge overnight. You will need to drain the mixture before assembling the wontons as there will be excess liquid.

Using a teaspoon of the mixture at a time, make into small balls. Heat the oil in a wok or large frypan and when it is hot add the balls. When they appear dark brown and float to the side they are ready. Drain and cool.

Boil some water in a pan and add the garlic chives for a couple of minutes, just to blanch. Remove and drain.

To assemble the wontons, place one wonton wrapper in your hand and then put another on top to make a star shape, then place the cooked ball in the centre. Pull the outside of the wrappers up to resemble a money bag and tie carefully with a stem of the garlic chive.

Using the leftover oil, cook the prepared wontons in the heated oil for 5–10 seconds until they turn golden brown.

Mix together the Peanut and Tartare Sauces and serve with the money bags.

Steak Tartare
Yook Hwe

Steak tartare makes a great entrée for your next dinner party or eaten tapas-style with a good wine.

200g (7oz) eye fillet
1 tablespoon Korean soy sauce
1 tablespoon minced garlic
1 teaspoon sugar
1 tablespoon sesame seeds
2 tablespoons sesame oil
1 spring onion (scallion), finely
   sliced
½ fuji apple or nashi pear
2 egg yolks

Put the fresh meat in the freezer for about 20 minutes or until semi-frozen, then slice it julienne-style as thinly as possible. Place meat in a mixing bowl and add soy sauce, garlic, sugar, sesame seeds, sesame oil and spring onion and mix together by hand.

Slice either the apple or pear in thin slices, divide onto two plates evenly in a mound shape, then gently place even amounts of the beef mixture on top of the mounds.

Put the egg yolks into spoons and place them on the plate next to the mixture.

Serve. To eat, simply combine all the ingredients together then eat straightaway.

Optional: Drizzle a little Bacardi 151 on the plate and light it up for an extra flair. You may torch the meat on top slightly if preferred.

Wagyu Dumplings
Mandu

Makes approximately 40

New Year's Day (lunar calendar) in Korea is when the family gathers together to make dumplings. Now I follow this tradition in my home and have my children help me—not quite the same and a lot messier but great fun. There is also an old myth that if you can make a pretty dumpling you will have a pretty daughter. I think I made beautiful dumplings!

500g (17½oz) wagyu, sirloin or
    chuck steak
100g (3½oz) sugar
250g (9oz) firm tofu
2 eggs
10g (⅓oz) fresh ginger
1 brown onion, finely sliced
25g (¾oz) garlic chives, finely
    sliced
100g (3½oz) cabbage, finely sliced
10ml (⅓fl oz) Korean or Japanese
    soy sauce
Pinch pepper
Pinch salt
1 tablespoon sugar
1 teaspoon minced garlic
1 teaspoon Korean beef stock
¼ cup plain (all-purpose) flour
1 pkt of 50 gow gee wrappers
Olive oil

SAUCE
1 tablespoon vinegar
1 tablespoon Korean or Japanese
    soy sauce
1 teaspoon sesame oil
1 teaspoon sesame seeds
1 tablespoon sugar

Cut the wagyu into cubes and soak in cold water for 15 minutes to remove the excess blood. Boil some water, add the meat and boil for 5 minutes. Discard the water, remove the meat and bring more water to the boil, then add the sugar and the meat. Once boiling, reduce the heat and simmer for one hour. When the meat has cooled, squeeze by hand into a mince.

In a blender or food processor, blend together tofu, egg and ginger until well combined, almost resembling a paste.

Add the onion, garlic chives and cabbage to the mince mixture and mix with your hands. Then add soy sauce, pepper, salt, sugar, garlic and beef stock and combine altogether.

Sprinkle a tray with plain flour and start making the dumplings. Stretch out the gow gee wrappers and then holding the wrapper in one hand, place a teaspoon of the mixture into the centre. With a little water on your finger, run around the edge of the wrapper. Carefully fold over and squeeze firmly in the centre. Starting on the left, fold over two flaps and then repeat on the right, making sure to press firmly, sealing the dumpling well to avoid meat escaping during cooking. Place the finished dumpling on the floured tray. Repeat until all the mixture has been used.

In a non-stick frypan, heat some olive oil to medium. When almost smoking, add a batch of dumplings and fry until brown on one side. Reduce the heat to low, add 2 tablespoons of water and cover the pan. When the water has evaporated and the skin is brown and crispy they are ready.

Mix all sauce ingredients together in a bowl and serve with your dumplings.

Tasty Japanese Scallops

Serves 2

Everyone knows scallops or has cooked them, but people say this dish is the best they have ever had. You will be a rock star at your own dinner party with this dish.

10 Japanese scallops, cleaned
Pinch salt
Pinch pepper
4 asparagus stems
2 tablespoons oil
½ tablespoon truffle oil
Teriyaki Sauce (see recipe)

Sprinkle the cleaned scallops with salt and pepper and leave for 5–10 minutes at room temperature, depending on how hot or cold your kitchen is.

Slice the asparagus into thin slices.

Heat the oil in a small frypan on a medium to high heat. Add the scallops and, when sizzling, turn them. The scallops should be brown on one side. Add the asparagus slices and when the scallop is browned on both sides it is ready.

The asparagus should remain a little crunchy—much better for you and much tastier.

When plated, drizzle with the truffle oil and teriyaki sauce.

Bean Curd With Lime Chilli Sauce

Serves 2

¼ brown onion, finely diced
100g (3½oz) kabocha or Japanese
    pumpkin, peeled and finely
    diced
2 eggs
400g (14oz) firm tofu
20 leaves Thai basil
Pinch salt
Pinch pepper
Potato starch (potato flour) for
    coating
Oil for deep-frying
Ginger Lime Sauce (see recipe)

Dice the onion and pumpkin finely and then add the eggs, tofu and basil with a pinch of salt and pepper. Mix together thoroughly with your hands and squeeze firmly.

Make patties in an oval shape and coat with the potato starch.

In a large saucepan heat the cooking oil on a medium heat until just boiling.

Deep-fry the tofu balls until golden brown, then remove and drain.

These are best served with the Ginger Lime Sauce.

If you wish, these can be oven-baked as an alternative.

mains

Bulgogi
Traditional Version

This dish reminds me of my mother as she would make it for me on my birthday and place it in the centre of the table surrounded by about 15 side dishes and right next to it, a big birthday cake. However, my friends and I could only ever remember eating half of it as it goes well with Korean soju—Korean rice wine with 24 per cent alcohol.

300g (10½oz) sirloin beef
1 onion
50g (1¾oz) nashi pear
2 tablespoons Korean soy sauce
1 tablespoon sesame oil
1 tablespoon sugar
½ tablespoon honey
1 tablespoon crushed garlic
½ teaspoon minced ginger
Pinch pepper
60ml (2fl oz) olive oil
½ tablespoon sesame seeds
Spring onion (scallion)
1 red pepper

Rinse the beef thoroughly under running water, then dry the excess water with cloths. Remove any excess fat and cut into thin slices. Cut the onion into slices about ½cm (⅛in) thick.

Blend the nashi pear and then combine it with soy sauce, sesame oil, sugar, honey, garlic, ginger and pepper. Add the beef and onion and, with gloves on, squeeze the marinade into the meat for about 5 minutes, then set aside for 30 minutes.

Heat the olive oil in a pan and add the sesame seeds, spring onion and red pepper and cook for 1 minute. Add the meat and marinade and toss until cooked.

I recommend you eat bulgogi wrapped in a fresh lettuce leaf accompanied with a little rice.

mains

Bulgogi
Modern Version

Serves 4

This is my version of slapping a steak on the barbecue.

1 nashi pear
1 onion
1kg (2lb 4oz) eye fillet
60ml (2fl oz) olive oil
Pinch salt
Pinch pepper
1 tablespoon butter
½ red onion, diced
200ml (7fl oz) red wine
50ml (1¾fl oz) raspberry cordial
50ml (1¾fl oz) sugar syrup
30ml (1fl oz) Korean soy sauce
1 medium zucchini (courgette)
4 stems broccolini
1 medium eggplant (aubergine)
½ red capsicum (bell pepper)

Blend the nashi pear and onion in a food processor to make a marinade for the beef. Divide the trimmed meat into 4 portions (250g/9oz each) sprinkle each piece with salt and pepper and pour over the pear and onion marinade. Leave in the fridge for at least 30 minutes.

In a frypan, melt the butter and then pan-fry the diced onion until soft. Add the wine, raspberry cordial, sugar syrup and soy sauce, then bring to the boil and simmer, uncovered, until it has a shiny appearance (approximately 15 minutes).

Pan-fry the meat on both sides to seal it, then grill on both sides turning only once.

Rest the meat in a VERY low oven for a maximum 10 minutes.

While the meat is resting, cut the zucchini, broccolini, eggplant and capsicum julienne-style in long pieces of around 10cm (4in) in length. Grill the vegetables.

Then add the meat to the simmering onion sauce for 10 seconds and return to the grill to mark the meat in crosses.

Place the meat on a plate and make a tower with the grilled vegetables. Drizzle a generous amount of onion sauce.

This is also great to eat with delicious Korean side dishes.

Bulgogi
Traditional Version

This dish reminds me of my mother as she would make it for me on my birthday and place it in the centre of the table surrounded by about 15 side dishes and right next to it, a big birthday cake. However, my friends and I could only ever remember eating half of it as it goes well with Korean soju—Korean rice wine with 24 per cent alcohol.

300g (10½oz) sirloin beef
1 onion
50g (1¾oz) nashi pear
2 tablespoons Korean soy sauce
1 tablespoon sesame oil
1 tablespoon sugar
½ tablespoon honey
1 tablespoon crushed garlic
½ teaspoon minced ginger
Pinch pepper
60ml (2fl oz) olive oil
½ tablespoon sesame seeds
Spring onion (scallion)
1 red pepper

Rinse the beef thoroughly under running water, then dry the excess water with cloths. Remove any excess fat and cut into thin slices. Cut the onion into slices about ½cm (⅛in) thick.

Blend the nashi pear and then combine it with soy sauce, sesame oil, sugar, honey, garlic, ginger and pepper. Add the beef and onion and, with gloves on, squeeze the marinade into the meat for about 5 minutes, then set aside for 30 minutes.

Heat the olive oil in a pan and add the sesame seeds, spring onion and red pepper and cook for 1 minute. Add the meat and marinade and toss until cooked.

I recommend you eat bulgogi wrapped in a fresh lettuce leaf accompanied with a little rice.

Bibimbap

This dish originates from the war days in Korea where a bit of 'whatever' food could be found was mixed with rice. There are no rules about what you can and can't put in a bibimbap—its direct translation to English is 'mixing rice' and that is exactly what we do.

2½ cups short-grain rice
2 carrots, peeled
Oil
Pinch salt
1 cup dried shiitake mushrooms
1 onion, peeled and sliced
1 bunch English spinach
2 cups bean sprouts
1 cucumber, sliced in lengths
   3 x ½cm (1⅛ x ⅛in)
4 eggs

ENGLISH SPINACH SEASONING
   SAUCE
½ tablespoon sesame oil
1 teaspoon Korean beef stock
½ teaspoon minced garlic

BEAN SPROUT SEASONING
   SAUCE
¼ tablespoon sesame oil
¼ tablespoon sesame seeds
Pinch salt

CHILLI SAUCE
100ml (3½fl oz) Korean chilli paste
3 teaspoons sugar syrup
20ml (⅔fl oz) sesame oil

In a bowl, wash the rice about four times or until the water seems clear, then cook in a rice cooker. If you do not have a rice cooker, put 3 cups of water from the final wash in a pot with the rice and heat for 4 minutes on a high heat. When it boils, continue on a medium heat for a further 3 minutes. Then lower the heat and simmer for 10 minutes.

Cut or grate the carrots into pieces about 3cm (1⅛in) in length, then stir-fry in a little oil and a pinch of salt until the carrot is just soft.

Soak the mushrooms in water for 30 minutes, drain and then pan-fry in a little oil with a pinch of salt until soft.

Stir-fry the onion in a little oil until soft but not brown.

Heat water in a saucepan and blanch the English spinach. Wash thoroughly to remove any sand and then squeeze out excess water with your hands and mix with the English spinach seasoning sauce.

Heat some water in a saucepan and, when boiling, add the bean sprouts and a pinch of salt and boil for 2 minutes. Drain and then add the bean sprout seasoning sauce, mixing with your hands.

Separate the egg whites and yolks into two bowls. Lightly beat both and in a small frypan (preferably square) put in a splash of oil and fry both yolks and whites separately. When cooled, cut into lengths of 3 x ½cm (1⅛ x ⅛in) wide.

In a bowl, mix the chilli paste, sugar syrup and sesame oil.

When all the ingredients are prepared it is now time to assemble the bibimbap. First, in a medium-sized bowl add 1 cup of cooked rice in the centre of the bowl. Now carefully place the ingredients in even amounts in a circle on top of the rice.

Fry the eggs and place on top of the bibimbap and drizzle a teaspoon of sesame oil over the ready meal.

Allow everyone to add the chilli sauce depending on their tastes, and mix it all together thoroughly.

Jaeyuk Gui
Modern Version

The coconut milk with the pork belly adds extra flavour and reduces the spice.

800g (1lb 12oz) pork belly
3 tablespoons white wine
2 tablespoons Korean chilli paste
1 tablespoon Korean chilli
    powder
1 tablespoon minced garlic
2 teaspoons minced ginger
1 tablespoon Korean soy sauce
4 tablespoons sugar syrup
Pinch pepper
2 tablespoons oil
5 tablespoons Ginger-flavoured
    Sweet Soy Sauce (see recipe)
1 kransky sausage, sliced
1 brown onion, sliced
1 red onion, sliced
2 spring onions (scallions), sliced
50g (1¾oz) Thai basil
½ cup bean sprouts, washed
3 birdseye chilli, chopped
50ml (1¾fl oz) coconut milk
3 red capsicums (bell peppers),
    for serving (optional)

Thinly slice the pork belly into bite-sized pieces, put into a bowl and pour over 1 tablespoon white wine. Set aside for 5 minutes. In a bowl, add the chilli paste, chilli powder, minced garlic, minced ginger, soy sauce, sugar syrup and pepper. Mix thoroughly by hand with gloves on. Add the pork belly and put the bowl in the fridge for 30 minutes.

Heat the oil in a frypan on a medium to high heat and add the pork belly, the remaining 2 tablespoons of white wine and the ginger-flavoured sweet soy sauce and then toss for 5 minutes. Remove from pan and place on a medium–high grill until the meat is marked.

Now add the kransky, onions, spring onions, Thai basil, bean sprouts and chilli to the frypan and toss with coconut milk until cooked. You may add some leftover marinade bit by bit if you need more juice, and depending on how much spice you can tolerate.

Remove the pork belly from the grill and you are ready to plate up. If you want to wow people with your presentation, use the capsicum.

Wash and cut the top and bottom off the capsicums, then put in a heated 220°C (430°F) oven for 5 minutes or until slightly softened.

I always place my pork belly and vegetable mix in the capsicum for a visual treat.

This is great with a bowl of steamed rice to mix with the tasty spicy sauce.

Jaeyuk Gui
Traditional Version

A quick and easy lunch for taxi drivers in Korea with a cup of soju.

300g (10½oz) pork neck
300g (10½oz) pork belly
1 tablespoon white wine
2 tablespoons Korean chilli paste
1 tablespoon Korean chilli
   powder
1 tablespoon minced garlic
2 teaspoons minced ginger
1 tablespoon Korean soy sauce
1 tablespoon sugar
3 tablespoons sugar syrup
1 teaspoon sesame oil
Pinch pepper
1 brown onion, sliced
2 spring onions (scallions), sliced
3 red peppers (chilli), sliced
2 tablespoons oil

Thinly slice the pork neck and belly into bite-sized pieces and pour the white wine over to marinate for 5 minutes.

In a mixing bowl, add the chilli paste, chilli powder, garlic, ginger, soy sauce, sugar, sugar syrup, sesame oil, pepper, onion, spring onions and chillies and mix together. Add the pork to the sauce and, wearing gloves, squeeze the sauce into the meat and leave in the fridge for 30 minutes or more.

Heat the oil in a frypan on a high heat, add the meat and toss. When the pork is sealed, add the remaining sauce and vegetables to the frypan, reduce the heat and cover for 5–10 minutes or until cooked through.

Turn off high again, remove the lid and toss the mixture, When the sauce has thickened and reduced it is ready.

This is best served with a bowl of steamed rice.

Whole Squid with a Korean/French Twist

Serves 2

In Korea, squid used to be really expensive so there was no waste—when mother bought a squid we ate the lot from top to bottom. This recipe isn't how we used to eat it but it's how I eat it now. This won't last long. YUM.

1 red capsicum (bell pepper), quartered

Pinch sea salt

Pinch pepper

3 tablespoons olive oil

10ml (1/3fl oz) squid ink

10g (1/3 oz) flour

10ml (1/3fl oz) water

1 red onion, finely diced

½ cucumber

2 mint leaves, finely chopped

10ml (1/3fl oz) lemon juice

1 whole squid

1 tablespoon butter

Preheat the oven to 180°C (350°F).

Using three-quarters of the capsicum, sprinkle with salt and pepper, drizzle with 1 tablespoon olive oil and cook in the oven for 20 minutes.

When it is cooked, remove from the oven and put in a blender to form a puree.

Combine the ink, flour and water and mix well. In the already heated oven, paint the mixture onto baking paper and bake for 5 minutes or until it becomes crispy.

Finely dice the red onion, cucumber, the remaining quarter-capsicum and the mint leaves. Combine together with pepper, salt and lemon juice to make a salsa.

Wash the squid and remove the head and legs, then carefully cut down one side of the tube and peel away the purple skin. Remove the 'guts' and carefully set aside the ink sac. Gently make criss-cross incisions in the tube and then cut the tube lengthways into 6 pieces. Finely dice the head and the legs.

In a large frypan on a high heat add the butter and cook the diced head and legs, tossing for about 3–4 minutes, then add the tubes and cook further on a high heat until ready. You know when the tubes are cooked when they start to form a shape and roll up. Be careful not to overcook as you don't want chewy squid. The best way is to taste-test the squid.

Serve on a large platter, paint on the pureed capsicum and squid ink amd then place the squid around the platter and top it with the salsa.

Crayfish with Gochujang Puree

Serves 2

Gochujang means 'chilli paste'. When I was growing up this was classed as 'hotel food' as only people staying in classy hotels could afford it!

600–800g (21–28oz) crayfish tail
   meat
Pinch salt
Pinch pepper
50g (1¾oz) butter

SALAD
½ green papaya
1 cup rocket
50ml (1¾oz) French Dressing (see
   recipe)

GOCHU JANG PUREE
50g (1¾oz) palm sugar
30ml (1fl oz) honey
100g (3½oz) Korean chilli paste
30ml (1fl oz) Lemon juice
10ml (¹/₃fl oz) lemon zest

Sprinkle the meat with salt and pepper and let stand for 5–10 minutes.

Heat the butter in a non-stick frypan and add the crayfish and cook on high on both sides for one minute on each side. Turn off the heat straightaway but leave the crayfish in the frypan for another minute on each side.

To make the salad, slice or grate the papaya into long thin lengths, add the washed rocket and toss with the French dressing.

To make the puree, melt the palm sugar in a pot over a low heat and then gradually add the honey. When this is melted and combined, add the chilli paste, lemon juice and lemon zest and stir over a low heat for around 5–10 minutes or until shiny.

The puree should be used to dip the meat into.

Crayfish can be quite expensive so shop around and buy when in season. I find the freshest and best by going to the local fish markets is the freshest and best.

Marinated Duck Breast

My mum tells me there is a special nutrient in duck meat that prevents you from suffering a stroke. This 'advice' is passed on from generation to generation and as duck is quite expensive in Seoul, whenever my mother comes to visit she makes me cook this particular dish for her MANY times.

100ml (3½oz) water
20ml (²/₃fl oz) Korean soy sauce
50g (1¾oz) palm sugar
1 cinnamon stick
4 bay leaves
4 meaty duck breasts with skin

SAUCE
300g (10½oz) cream
1 bunch Thai basil
½ onion, chopped
2 tablespoons butter
2 tablespoons palm sugar

Place the water, soy sauce and palm sugar into a saucepan and bring to the boil. When it is boiling, add the cinnamon stick and bay leaves, and turn the heat off and allow to cool to room temperature. Use this mixture to marinate the duck for approximately one hour.

Preheat the oven to 220°C (430°F). Place the marinated duck on a roasting pan and cook in the oven for about 10 minutes or until the skin is crispy. Turn off the oven and leave the duck inside for 2 minutes.

Place the sauce ingredients into a blender and combine well. Pour into a saucepan and simmer for 10 minutes.

Plate up the duck and either drizzle the sauce over it or serve as a dipping sauce on the plate.

Serve the duck with your choice of salad or vegetables.

Coffee Pork Ribs

Serves 4

This is now our signature dish at Mapo—thanks to my mother when she was visiting me once. We took her to a pub for a meal and shared some pork ribs with her. She said they smelt and that she could do better. So back we went to Mapo for her to cook up this amazing dish.

2 litres (70fl oz) water
100g (3½oz) instant coffee
1 onion
1.5kg (3lb 5oz) pork ribs

TERIYAKI SAUCE
5 cups water
1 cup Korean soy sauce
1 cup soju or moselle wine
½ cup sugar
2 cups sugar syrup
3 big pieces of fresh ginger

½ iceberg lettuce

In a large saucepan, bring the water to the boil and add the instant coffee and whole peeled onion. Reduce the heat and add the pork ribs. Simmer for about 2 hours or until the meat begins to look shiny, like jelly.

Turn off the heat and leave in the saucepan overnight to cool down.

In the meantime, make the teriyaki sauce. In a medium-sized saucepan, bring the water to the boil and add all the ingredients. Reduce the heat and simmer for about 20 minutes or until the ginger has become smaller. Put in the fridge to cool.

When you are ready to eat, add the pre-made teriyaki sauce to a frypan and heat slowly, then add the pieces of pork ribs. When warmed through they are ready to eat.

To make them even tastier I recommend putting the ribs on a preheated grill to finish them off.

Wash the iceberg lettuce and separate the leaves. This is all you need to accompany the tasty pork ribs.

Crispy Skin Pork Belly

In Korea we usually eat pork skin while it is soft but after experiencing a crispy roast pork at my in-laws I now know it is definitely best crunchy!

1kg (2lb 4oz) pork belly
1 tablespoon salt
1 teaspoon whole pepper seeds
1 cup cooking red wine
4 bay leaves

SAUCE
100g (3½oz) doenjang paste
   (Korean fermented soybean
   paste)
50g (1¾oz) Korean chilli paste
50ml (1¾fl oz) plum wine
2 tablespoons minced garlic
2 tablespoons sesame oil
2 tablespoons sesame seeds

Leaving the pork belly whole, sprinkle the meaty side with the salt then place on a roasting pan with the skin facing up and sprinkle the pepper seeds on top. Pour the red wine into the tray with the bay leaves, not allowing any ingredients to touch the skin except the pepper. Put in the fridge to marinate for at least two hours.

Preheat the oven to 220°C (430°F).

On another clean oven tray, line it with baking paper and place on the marinated pork belly, this time with the skin facing down. Lay another sheet of baking paper across the top of the meat.

You will need to use a stone or something heavy to push down the baking paper while still keeping it even.

Check every 30 minutes, replacing the baking paper each time, turning the meat over and pressing it down where required. You will probably have to repeat this about three or four times. You will know when the pork is cooked when the skin is crispy.

The sauce is simple to make, just mix everything together.

I would recommend serving this with some Korean Pickled Vegetables (see recipe).

Salmon Fillet

Serves 4

I have been fortunate enough to attend a lot of weddings where, at the dinner, I have been offered a choice of salmon or steak. So I decided it was time to create an interesting salmon dish.

800g (28oz) fresh Atlantic salmon
¼ cup white wine
Pinch pepper
Pinch salt
2 tablespoons olive oil

SAUCE
1 dragonfruit
4 tablespoons lemon juice
4 tablespoons white wine
6 tablespoons sugar
2 tablespoons balsamic vinegar

SALSA
½ dragonfruit, finely diced
½ cucumber, finely diced
½ brown onion, finely diced
½ avocado, finely diced
1 tablespoon lemon juice
Pinch sugar
Pinch salt

Preheat oven to 220°C (430°F).

Marinate all the salmon pieces in the white wine, pepper and salt for 20 minutes.

Meanwhile, make a tasty dragonfruit sauce. Squeeze the whole dragonfruit by hand to juice it into a small saucepan. Place it over a low heat and add in the lemon juice, white wine, sugar and balsamic vinegar and simmer until it is reduced and sticky with a glazed appearance.

Now heat the olive oil in a hot pan and add the salmon fillet with the skin side down until it is crispy or cooked halfway. You will know this by simply looking at the salmon.

Remove the salmon and place on a lined baking tray skin side up. Cook for a further 5–10 minutes depending on how you like to eat your salmon.

While this is in the oven, you can prepare your dragonfruit salsa by tossing together the dragonfruit, cucumber, onion and avocado and then toss it with the lemon juice, sugar and salt.

To serve, carefully place the salmon on the plate, drizzle with the dragonfruit sauce and place a mound of salsa beside the salmon.

Salmon with Wasabi Mayonnaise

Serves 4

This is my salmon dish with a strong Japanese influence.

800g (28oz) salmon fillet
30ml (1fl oz) olive oil
1 cup white wine
80g (2½oz) sea salt
1 tablespoon ground pepper

WASABI MAYONNAISE
100g (3½oz) Korean or Japanese
  mayonnaise
50g (1¾oz) sugar
30g (1oz) wasabi powder
30ml (1fl oz) lime juice
20ml (⅔fl oz) lemon juice

ORANGE ZEST
2 oranges
50g (1¾oz) sugar
1 cup orange juice

Preheat the oven to the lowest temperature.

Slice the salmon into bite-sized pieces and drizzle the olive oil, wine, sea salt and pepper on top. Leave for 20 minutes at room temperature.

Place salmon on a lined baking tray and bake in the oven for 10–20 minutes until the salmon is only just cooked in the middle. Remove from the oven and it is ready to serve.

Meanwhile, make the mayonnaise by mixing all ingredients together.

To make the orange zest, remove the peel and slice the orange peel into thin pieces. Put the orange peel, sugar and juice in a pan and bring to a simmer. Cook until the mixture appears shiny and sticky.

To serve, place the salmon in the centre of the plate and drizzle the orange zest in a circle around the edge of the plate. Pour the mayonnaise in a mound so it can be dipped into.

Curry-flavoured Fish

Serves 2

I like to cook this as the quality of the fish I can get is world-class—it is meaty and so fresh. This is one of my favourite dishes to cook. It's quite simple but very tasty.

2 snapper or bream fillets
Pinch salt
Pinch pepper
20g (²/₃oz) plain flour
10g (¹/₃oz) Korean curry powder
1 tablespoon oil

SAUCE
1 tablespoon oil
2 birdseye chillies, finely diced
½ red onion, finely diced
1 teaspoon fresh ginger, finely diced
2 cloves garlic, finely diced
2 tablespoons Korean or Japanese soy sauce
2 tablespoons oyster sauce
4 tablespoons sweet white wine
4 tablespoons white vinegar
Pinch pepper

Place the fish in a bowl and sprinkle with salt and pepper. Refrigerate for 10 minutes.

Preheat the oven to 170°C (340°F).

Combine the plain flour and curry powder together and coat the fish. Heat the oil in a large frypan and cook the fish on a low heat until it is a light brown on each side. Place the fish on a lined baking tray and cook for 10 minutes, uncovered.

To make the sauce, heat the oil in a frypan and fry the chillies, onion, ginger and garlic, then add the soy sauce, oyster sauce, wine, vinegar and pepper. Once it is boiling, reduce the heat and simmer until the sauce becomes thick.

By this time the fish should be ready to take out of the oven.

Place each fish on a dinner plate and drizzle generously with the sauce. This is best served with a bowl of steamed rice.

Chung Jae's Fish

Serves 2

This is my own creation with an amazing fish. We don't get barramundi in Korea and my favourite fish to cook used to be ribbon fish, which has a similar taste but is not quite as good as this. If you can't find barramundi, use a white, flaky fish.

500g (17½oz) barramundi fillet or
   2 fillets
Pinch sea salt
Pinch ground pepper
2 tablespoons oil
1 tablespoon butter
10 fresh cockles (Goolwa, pipis or
   any local variety)
1 bunch bok choy
1 tablespoon oil
2 tablespoons minced garlic
50ml (1¾fl oz) water
2 tablespoons sesame oil
Pinch salt
4 tablespoons Choo Chee Sauce
   (see recipe)

On the cleaned fillets carefully mark the skin with a sharp knife about 1cm (⅓in) deep, then sprinkle with salt and pepper and leave sitting out at room temperature for 30 minutes, covered. Heat the oil in a frypan on high heat, then add the fish skin down, pushing down for about 10 seconds and reducing the heat to medium immediately. When the fish is half cooked, turn on the other side. When the juice is sizzling from the skin, add the butter and cockles and cook for a further 3–4 minutes or until everything is cooked.

Clean and cut the bok choy in quarters. Heat the oil in a pan and add the garlic first, then when you can smell the garlic cooking add the bok choy and water. Simmer until the water has almost disappeared, then add the sesame oil and salt and quickly toss.

To serve this, put a generous circle of the choo chee sauce on a large plate and then add the fish and cockles topped with the bok choy.

Spicy Seafood

Serves 2

I love this one, except I add a bit more chilli as I need spice and a lot of it. When I go out for breakfast the waiting staff always look at me strangely when I ask for hot chilli to go with my eggs and bacon.

2 squid tubes
16 black shell mussels
12 prawn (shrimp) cutlets
8 half-shell mussels
5 tablespoons olive oil
1 teaspoon minced garlic
4 bay leaves
1 red chilli, sliced
½ red onion, sliced
4 tablespoons Korean chilli
   powder
1 cup cabbage, sliced
10 leaves Thai basil
½ cup water
30ml (1fl oz) Korean soy sauce
60ml (2fl oz) sugar syrup
1 tablespoon sugar
Pinch pepper and salt
6 scallops
1 spring onion (scallion), finely
   chopped

Put squid and black shell mussels in cold water with a pinch of salt for 10 minutes. Clean the mussels and slice the squid into slices about ½cm (¼in). Wash the prawns and devein. Clean the half-shell mussels and set aside all seafood.

Heat 3 tablespoons oil in a large frypan and add garlic, bay leaves and red chilli. When they turn brown add the black and half shell mussels. Be careful as this may spit due to the mix of water and oil, so reduce the heat and place a lid on the pan and steam the mussels until they open. Remove them from the pan and set aside.

To the mussel sauce, add in the onion, chilli powder, cabbage and basil, water, Korean soy sauce, sugar syrup, sugar and pepper and salt. Cook for 2–3 minutes or until the vegetables are softened.

In another frypan, heat 2 tablespoons olive oil and when hot add the squid. When the squid begins to curl and shrink add the scallops and prawns. When the prawns turn a light orange colour, take off the heat and add to the sauce mixture along with the mussels and chopped spring onion. Mix everything together thoroughly and it is now ready.

This is best served with a nice bowl of freshly cooked steamed rice.

Seafood Pancake
Haemalpajan

This dish reminds me of a rainy day in Korea as this is what we used to eat for afternoon tea with friends while sipping on one of our rice wines, Mokoli.

95g (3¹/₃oz) plain flour
30g (1oz) sticky rice
200g (7oz) water
3 eggs
1 teaspoon salt
Pinch pepper
2 teaspoons Korean beef stock
7 prawns (shrimp)
1 squid tube
5 pieces scallop
1 zucchini (courgette)
1 bunch garlic chives
85g (3oz) oil
1 bunch spring onion (scallions),
   thinly sliced in rounds
100g (3½oz) crab meat

SAUCE
20g (²/₃oz) Korean soy sauce
1 teaspoon sesame oil
1 tablespoon minced garlic
2 teaspoons sugar
1 teaspoon toasted sesame seeds

In a large mixing bowl combine the plain flour, sticky rice, water, eggs, salt, pepper and Korean beef stock. Whisk until the ingredients are well combined.

Wash the prawns in cold salty water and drain. Then finely chop the squid and wash in cold water with the scallops and drain.

Cut the zucchini julienne-style and finely dice the chives then add to the flour mixture.

Heat a large flat frypan, add oil and cook the spring onions for 30 seconds. Add half of the seafood and toss for about one minute. Reduce the heat to low and add half the flour and egg mixture. When the pancake starts to brown it is ready. Turn it once.

Repeat for the second pancake.

Combine all the sauce ingredients together and serve in a small bowl.

Tuna with Fried Kimchi

Serves 2

People love to eat tuna raw or seared but to me it lacks taste until I add kimchi—then it becomes a memorable dish.

250g (9oz) fresh tuna fillets
Pinch salt
Pinch pepper
50g (1¾oz) toasted sesame seeds
3 tablespoons olive oil
100g (3½oz) kimchi
1 tablespoon sugar
1 tablespoon sesame oil
50ml (1¾fl oz) coconut milk
2 sprigs of chives

Preheat the oven to 180°C (350°F).

Sprinkle the tuna with salt and pepper and leave for 15 minutes at room temperature.

Coat the tuna in the toasted sesame seeds. Heat 2 tablespoons oil in frypan, low–medium heat, and cook the tuna until the sesame seeds appear dark brown. Turn on the other side and repeat.

Place the tuna on baking paper on a baking tray and put in the oven to finish cooking.

How long you cook it for is up to you. I prefer it still raw in the middle, not cooked all the way through, so usually 3–4 minutes in the oven is enough for me.

Drain the kimchi, keeping the juice separate, and dice finely. Heat remaining 1 tablespoon oil and fry the kimchi until golden brown, adding the sugar and sesame oil just before the kimchi is browned.

In a saucepan, add the kimchi juice and coconut milk and bring to the boil. Once boiling, reduce the heat and simmer for 10 minutes. This is your kimchi puree.

Spread the kimchi puree around your plate, put a pile of half of the fried kimchi in the centre of the plate and then carefully place the tuna on top.

Lay one chive across the top of each tuna steak.

Crispy Tempura Shrimp

Serves 4

An all-time favourite for everyone, this is tempura my way.

20 whole prawns (shrimp),
   medium to large
1 cup tempura powder
2 tablespoons potato starch
   (potato flour)
3 cups iced water
Pinch salt
Pinch pepper
1 egg yolk
3–4 cups oil
Tartare Sauce (see recipe)

Use a toothpick to devein the prawns.

In a bowl, add the tempura powder and coat the prawns. Set aside the prawns and add to the tempura powder the potato starch, iced water, salt and pepper. Mix well and then add the egg yolk to make a tempura batter. Coat the prawns in the batter.

In a wok or large frypan, heat the oil on a medium heat for about 10 minutes. To test it sprinkle a little batter in—if it sizzles you know it's ready. Add the prawns. When they float and go to the side of the pan and appear golden brown they are ready.

My own special tartare sauce is great for dipping the prawns in.

Kimchi Fried Rice

Serves 2

My mum is the best at this dish but she likes chilli a lot and makes it so spicy that not everyone can handle it, so lucky for me I get a big serving. This is so good and so simple—just don't plan on kissing anyone straight after eating it!

2 cups kimchi
5 rashers bacon
½ brown onion
1 squid tube
1 tablespoon oil
1 tablespoon Korean chilli paste
Pinch Korean beef stock
2 cups cooked rice
50g (1¾oz) dried fried onions
100g (3½oz) bean sprouts
Pinch salt
Pepper
1 tablespoon sesame oil
½ tablespoon sesame seeds
2 eggs

Dice the kimchi, bacon, onion and squid. In a large frypan add the oil and fry the bacon and squid with the kimchi and onion together on a high heat until browned. Add the chilli paste and beef stock and combine together. Then add the rice and mix thoroughly for 2 minutes. Next, add the dried onions, bean sprouts, salt and pepper and cook for 30 seconds, still on a high heat.

Add the sesame oil and sesame seeds and stir through.

In a separate frypan, fry the eggs.

Divide the mixture over two plates in mounds and decorate with the fried egg sitting on top.

Tempura Chicken
Kangpoong Ki

Serves 4

This is my version of Kangpoong Ki, which is a dish found in Chinese restaurants throughout Korea, with tempura chicken swimming in spicy sauce. I have changed this a bit as I like my chicken lightly battered and crispy.

600g (21oz) chicken breast
100ml (3½fl oz) soju or sake or
  white wine
2 egg yolks
1 litre (36fl oz) cold water
Oil
½ cup tempura powder
Salt and pepper
Honey Mustard Dressing (see
  recipe)

Cut the chicken into pieces about ½cm (⅛in) wide and marinate in the soju for 30 minutes.

Whisk the egg yolks and water together and put in the fridge to chill. The colder the batter the better, to ensure that your chicken stays moist on the inside and crunchy on the outside.

In a wok or large frypan, heat the oil on a slow heat for about 15 minutes. To test if it is ready, sprinkle a little salt—if it sizzles the oil is hot enough.

Add the tempura powder to the egg yolk and water, whisking together to form the tempura batter.

Add the chicken pieces to the batter ensuring to coat well. Now put the chicken in the hot oil and it should be cooked in 5–6 minutes. You will know when it is ready as the pieces will float to the top and then to the side, turning a lovely golden brown.

The dressing can either be served as a dipping sauce or drizzled over the chicken. A fresh garden salad best accompanies this dish.

Chilli Chicken
Dakgalbi

Serves 4

This is a popular dish for university students as it is less expensive than some other meals and also great to enjoy with a nice bottle of soju.

4 chicken thigh fillets, skin off
150g (5oz) cabbage
1 brown onion
2 spring onions (scallions)
100g (3½oz) sweet potato
1 red chilli
1 green chilli
2 tablespoons oil
4 cups cooked rice

MARINADE
½ onion
3 tablespoons Korean chilli
   powder
2 tablespoons sugar
2 tablespoons white wine
   (Moselle)
1 tablespoon Korean or Japanese
   soy sauce
1 tablespoon Korean curry
   powder
1 tablespoon minced garlic
½ tablespoon minced ginger
½ tablespoon sesame oil
Pinch pepper
3 tablespoons sugar syrup

Carefully cut the chicken into bite-sized pieces.

To make the marinade, blitz the onion in a food processor to form a juice, then mix in the rest of the ingredients. Pour over the chicken and leave for 1½ hours.

Wash and cut the cabbage, onion and spring onions into small square shapes. Thinly slice the sweet potato and the red and green chilli.

Heat the oil in a large frypan and fry the chicken. Add in all the vegetables and cook for about 15 minutes or until ready.

Serve equally into 4 bowls. Once all the chicken has been eaten, add the cooked rice and mix with the remaining spicy sauce. Yum!

Soy Chicken Drumsticks

Serves 2–3

Eating fried chicken is popular in all cultures and I particularly like the drumstick as I like the meat close to the bone. It is usually quite fatty so I have tried to create a dish with less calories and more taste.

10 drumsticks
1 litre (36fl oz) milk
2 tablespoons oil

MARINADE
120ml (4fl oz) Korean soy sauce
2 tablespoons oyster sauce
2 tablespoons sugar
1 tablespoon plum wine
1 tablespoon sesame oil
1 tablespoon minced ginger
2 tablespoons minced garlic
2 tablespoons white wine
Pinch pepper
1 tablespoon thick caramel sauce
   (also known as Chinese dark soy
   sauce, available in supermarkets
   and Asian grocers)
1 tablespoon sesame seeds

PICKLED RADISH
400g (14oz) Chinese radish
½ cup water
½ cup sugar
½ cup white vinegar
1 tablespoon salt

With a sharp knife, stab each of the chicken drumsticks about four times anywhere in the meaty bit, and then soak in the milk for one hour.

Mix all the marinade ingredients together except for the sesame seeds.

When the hour is up, drain the milk from the chicken drumsticks.

In a wok or large frypan, heat up the oil and, reducing the heat to medium, add the chicken drumsticks and start cooking. Once the chicken is sealed, add the remaining marinade and put the lid on, reducing the heat to low. After about 15 minutes remove the lid and if the sauce has reduced they are ready to eat. When the heat is turned off, scatter over the sesame seeds and toss.

Whenever Koreans eat fried chicken it is a necessity to eat it with pickled radish. Even if we have a home delivery of fried chicken it will always come with the radish.

Dice the radish into small bite-sized cubes and place in the water, sugar, vinegar and salt. This is best made one day before but can be eaten on the same day.

Potato Noodles
Japchae

This is one of my personal favourites. We always eat it at family functions, whether we are celebrating a birthday, Christmas or the birthday of a deceased member of a family.

   The potato noodles are long noodles and when eaten at the birth of a baby this means a long life. I would suggest you get your kids to wash the dishes as there are a lot to do after making these delicious noodles.

½ cup dried shiitake mushrooms
½ cup Swiss brown mushrooms
⅓ carrot
½ cucumber
2 pinches salt
1 onion, peeled
30g (1oz) bean sprouts
2 eggs
30g (1oz) English spinach
60g (2oz) potato starch (potato
   flour) noodles

SEASONING SAUCE
½ tablespoon soy sauce
½ tablespoon sugar
¼ tablespoon sesame oil
¼ tablespoon sesame seeds
Pinch salt

ENGLISH SPINACH SEASONING
   SAUCE
½ tablespoon sesame oil
1 teaspoon Korean beef stock
½ teaspoon minced garlic

BEAN SPROUTS SEASONING
   SAUCE
Pinch salt
½ teaspoon sesame oil

Soak the shiitake mushrooms in water for about an hour, then finely slice them julienne-style. Over a low-medium heat, toss the shiitake mushrooms lightly in a frypan with the seasoning sauce until coated. Remove the mushrooms. Add the finely sliced Swiss brown mushrooms to the pan and fry until cooked.

Peel the carrot and cucumber and slice into lengths of about 5cm (2in) and about 0.3cm (⅛in) wide, then marinate in salt for 5 minutes. Wash off salt and set aside.

Peel the onion and cut into a similar size to the carrot and cucumber. Wash the bean sprouts and set aside.

Lightly beat the eggs with a pinch of salt and cook on both sides in a flat frypan over a low heat until just cooked. Let cool and then slice into lengths of 5cm (2in) and 0.3cm (⅛in) wide.

NOODLE SEASONING SAUCE
½ tablespoon soy sauce
½ teaspoon sugar
½ teaspoon minced garlic
1 teaspoon sesame oil
Pinch pepper
1 teaspoon Korean beef stock

Heat water in a saucepan and blanch the English spinach. Wash thoroughly to remove any sand and then squeeze out excess water. Mix with the English spinach seasoning sauce.

Heat a large frypan with oil and stir-fry the mushrooms and onion for 2 minutes over medium heat. Remove from the pan and set aside. Stir-fry the carrot and the cucumber in the same pan for 30 seconds on a high heat.

Bring some water in a saucepan to the boil and then add the bean sprouts, scalding with a pinch of salt for 2 minutes. Drain and then add the bean sprouts seasoning sauce and mix with your hands.

In a large pot boil some water, add the noodles and boil for about 8 minutes, then drain and cut into 20cm (8in) lengths. Mix with the noodle seasoning sauce.

Now finally heat a large saucepan and stir-fry the noodles for 2 minutes, then add all other ingredients and mix well together. This dish is traditionally served at room temperature but can be eaten straightaway.

Bossam Kimchi with Pork Belly

This dish reminds me of my childhood. Every couple of months, my mother would make a fresh batch of kimchi and the neighbours would cook some pork belly. We would then combine the dishes and eat the meal together.

1 apple, sliced into rounds

1 stem fresh ginger, peeled and sliced into rounds

1 garlic head, peeled and sliced into rounds

1 onion, sliced into rounds

Oil

1 teaspoon whole peppercorn

3 bay leaves

2kg (4lb 6oz) pork belly

20g (²/₃oz) Korean soy sauce

200ml (7fl oz) soju

500ml (17½fl oz) water

400g (14oz) dried radish

2 tablespoons salt

100g (3½oz) sugar

2 cups water

1 Chinese cabbage

10 cups water

2 cups coarse salt

100ml (3½fl oz) fish sauce

300ml (10½fl oz) sugar syrup

½ cup minced garlic

½ cup Korean chilli powder

1 bunch Chinese chives

Slice the apple, ginger, garlic and onion into rounds. In a deep saucepan add enough oil to line the bottom of the pan.

Carefully layer the bottom of the pan with the sliced apple, ginger, garlic, onion, pepper and bay leaves.

Lay the pork belly on top and add the soy sauce and soju, then slowly add the water until it covers half of the pork.

On a medium heat gently bring it to the boil, then cover and reduce the heat to simmer for approximately 2.5 hours, checking every 30 minutes and adding small amounts of water as required.

After about 2 hours insert a skewer into the meat and if it comes out clean turn off the heat.

Once you have cooked the meat, drain it and allow to cool. Slice the meat and place in a bowl with the dried radish, salt, sugar and water and leave for about an hour or until the radish seems swollen. Drain and squeeze out the excess water but do not rinse.

While the radish is soaking, cut the cabbage into four even pieces. This is done by cutting longways into quarters.

In a large bowl, add about 10 cups water (enough to cover the 4 cabbage pieces) and add the salt. You can check if there is enough salt by placing an egg into the water—if it floats you have enough salt. If it sinks add a little more salt until the egg floats.

Then add the cabbage and leave for 30–45 minutes or until the cabbage is floppy! When it is ready, drain the cabbage and wash the salt out thoroughly. You may need to taste a little bit to make sure it is not too salty. Squeeze the excess water out with your hands.

Combine the fish sauce, sugar syrup, garlic, chilli powder and finely sliced Chinese chives. Then when ready add the prepared cabbage and radish and give it a good mix together with your hands.

Remove the pork and cut into pieces around 1 x 1cm (¼ x ¼in).

Serve the pork and kimchi on a plate together. It should be eaten by wrapping the pork in the cabbage leaf. You can accompany with a bowl of rice if you wish.

Chunky Beef

Serves 4

Here is my version of beef stew. This is one of my wife's favourite dishes as it is so tasty with a little bit of sweetness.

1kg (2lb 4oz) beef brisket or any
    sort of stewing steak
14 cups water
2 brown onions, sliced
1 cup sugar
1 carrot
10 quail eggs (tinned or fresh)
½ cup Korean soy sauce
Splash soju
Pinch pepper
1½ tablespoons minced garlic
1 teaspoon minced ginger
1 tablespoon sugar syrup
½ cup spring onion (scallions)
1 bundle of bok choy

Trim the beef and cut into pieces approximately 3.5 x 3.5cm (1⅓ x 1⅓in). Bring to the boil 4 cups of water in a pot and boil the beef for approximately 10 minutes. Discard the water and set aside the beef.

Boil 10 cups of water, then add the meat and simmer for a further 2 hours. Add the onion and sugar to the meat and continue to simmer.

After 2 hours the water should be substantially reduced.

Slice the carrot julienne-style and add to the meat with quail eggs, Korean soy sauce, soju, pepper, minced garlic, minced ginger and sugar syrup.

Wash and cut the spring onions and bok choy and when the carrot is tender it is time to add them too.

When the sauce looks shiny you are ready to eat this tasty dish.

Eat with a bowl of freshly cooked steamed rice and kimchi.

Kimchi Noodles
Kimchi Bibim Guk Su

 Serves 2

This dish is great in summer on a really hot day. There are usually lines of people who want to get into Guk Su restaurants in Korea at lunch during summer, as Koreans believe eating spicy food when it is hot helps to reduce their body temperature.

4 litres water (135fl oz)
300g (10½oz) wheat noodles (thin vermicelli)
1 egg
3 tablespoons gochujang (Korean chilli paste)
3 tablespoons honey
1 tablespoon white vinegar
1 tablespoon sesame oil
1 tablespoon sesame seeds
½ tablespoon Korean chilli powder
½ fuji apple
300g (10½oz) Kimchi (see recipe)

Bring 2 litres (70fl oz) of water to the boil in a large pot, then add the noodles the same as you would add pasta, in a circular clockwise motion. When the water is boiling again, add one cup room-temperature water and repeat one more time when the water reboils. To know when the noodles are ready, either taste them or put a few strands into cold water and if they are no longer firm they are ready.

In a separate saucepan, boil the egg until it is hard-boiled.

Drain the noodles with cold water and set aside.

In a bowl, mix together the chilli paste, honey, vinegar, sesame oil, sesame seeds and chilli powder. Slice the apple and peel the egg.

Cut the egg in half lengthways. In 2 large bowls, divide the noodles evenly and top with equal amounts of the kimchi. Now pour over the sauce to your desired amount and decorate with the sliced apple and boiled egg.

Before eating, give the dish a good stir through.

Beef and Pork Patties
Yukwonjeon

This is a simple recipe and is one of my favourite dishes to have with rice. My mother is the master of this one.

1 brown onion, finely diced
100g (3½oz) beef mince
100g (3½oz) pork mince
50g (1¾oz) firm tofu
2 eggs
½ teaspoon ginger
⅔ teaspoon soy sauce
Pinch salt and pepper
1 teaspoon sugar
1 teaspoon garlic
3 tablespoons plain flour
Oil

SAUCE
1 tablespoon Korean or Japanese
   soy sauce
1 tablespoon white vinegar
1 tablespoon water

Using your hands, mix the onion through and combine with the beef and pork mince and the tofu. Add 1 egg and mix thoroughly, then add ginger, soy sauce, salt, pepper, sugar and garlic. In a small bowl, beat the remaining egg. Put the flour on a separate plate.

Make the mixture into small balls about the size of a walnut. This is easier with a trickle of oil on your hands as the mixture won't stick. Coat in flour and then dip into the beaten egg.

Heat oil in pan and pan-fry the patties on a medium heat for 4 minutes on one side and another 3 minutes on the other side, or until cooked through.

It is easiest to combine the sauce ingredients together by putting them in a shaker. Drizzle the sauce over the patties to serve.

Chung Jae's Family Lamb Cutlets

Serves 4

Cutlets are unavailable to purchase in Korea, and knowing how my in-laws enjoy lamb I created this dish just for them.

2 tablespoons soy sauce
50ml (1¾fl oz) soju
2 tablespoons sugar syrup
2 big pinches pepper
1 tablespoon sesame oil
1 tablespoon BBQ sauce
8 lamb cutlets or chops
1 tablespoon oil
½ sweet potato, peeled and
   sliced julienne-style
1 bunch broccoli, washed and
   chopped into small pieces
3 tablespoons fried shallots
2 tablespoons soy sauce
4 tablespoons sugar syrup
50ml (1¾fl oz) cream

In a bowl, mix together the soy sauce, soju, sugar syrup, pepper, sesame oil and BBQ sauce. Coat the lamb cutlets in the mixture for an hour to marinate.

Once marinated, simply grill the cutlets to your liking.

In a frypan heat the oil, then add the sweet potato and fry until half cooked. Add the broccoli, fried shallots, soy sauce, sugar syrup and cream.

I'm told this dish goes well with a nice cold beer!

Kimbap

This is perfect for a picnic lunch on a beautiful spring day. Korean mothers always make this for sports day—it has the right amount of carbohydrates to keep the kids at their best.

200g (7oz) beef mince (ground beef)
1 cucumber
3 eggs
Pinch salt and pepper
1 tablespoon oil
1 carrot
1 tablespoon oil
Pinch salt
3 bowls cooked medium-grain rice
4 pieces of seaweed (sushi)
4 strips yellow radish

MINCE SAUCE
2½ tablespoons Korean soy sauce
1½ tablespoons sugar
1 teaspoon minced garlic
1 tablespoon sesame oil
1½ tablespoons soju or white wine
3 tablespoons sugar syrup
Pinch pepper
Pinch salt

RICE SAUCE
½ tablespoon Korean beef stock
1 tablespoon sesame oil
1 tablespoon sesame seeds

Wrap the mince in a kitchen towel to remove any excess juice. In a mixing bowl add the mince and all the sauce ingredients—soy sauce, sugar, minced garlic, sesame oil, soju, sugar syrup, pepper and salt—and mix together with your hands.

Pan-fry on a high heat (there is no need to add additional oil) until cooked and then set aside.

Slice the cucumber in thin slices, removing the seeds as they make the sushi soggy. Set aside.

Whisk the eggs, salt and pepper. In a frypan heat the oil on a low heat and add the egg mixture, trying to form a rectangle shape if possible. Slowly cook this on both sides then set aside. When this is cooled and cut into lengths as long as the piece of seaweed and about 1cm (⅓in) thick.

Peel the carrot and cut julienne-style about 4cm (1½in) in length and ½cm (⅛in) thick. In a frypan, heat the oil and fry the carrot until soft. Sprinkle with salt and don't overcook as you want to ensure the colour stays vibrant.

Combine the ingredients for the rice suace and then add this to the cooked rice and toss through.

Lay out the seaweed onto a sushi mat and spread a quarter of the rice evenly over the whole sheet.

In the middle of the half closest to you, carefully place a quarter of the mince mixture, the cucumber, egg omelette, carrot and radish and roll it, pressing firmly but not too hard, ensuring the rice makes the sushi seal.

Set aside and repeat with the remaining three seaweed pieces.

Spread a little bit of sesame oil on a sharp knife as this will make it easier to cut the rolls.

First cut in the middle, then cut each half into 4 pieces making 8 pieces per roll.

I like adding Korean chilli paste (gochujang) to this as it gives it a bit of a kick.

Mains

BBQ

Beef Short Ribs

Serves 4

This is a beautiful tender cut of meat that is fantastic to barbecue and very famous throughout South Korea.

4kg (8lb 13oz) beef short ribs
2 onions, peeled
1 large nashi pear
2 fuji apples
1 cup soy sauce
5 tablespoons sesame oil
1 tablespoon pepper
80g (2½oz) minced garlic
½ cup sugar
½ kiwi fruit

To purchase the meat it is best to go to a Korean butcher. If you don't have one in your local area, go to your regular butcher and ask them to 'butterfly cut' the ribs for you.

In a blender, add the onions, nashi pear and apples and make into a juice.

In a mixing bowl, add the soy sauce, sesame oil, pepper, minced garlic, sugar and the juice of the kiwi fruit and mix thoroughly together, then add the juice from the onions, pear and apples and now you have your marinade.

Place a rib on a sheet of aluminum foil, spread the marinade heavily covering one side of the rib and then roll it up. Repeat with all the ribs, then put them in an airtight container and leave in the fridge for at least 24 hours—two days is better.

To cook these ribs just grill them on the barbecue. They go well with soju (Korea's national drink).

Korean-inspired Lamb Shashliks

Serves 4

Koreans don't eat much lamb at all and I'm not a big fan of lamb except for this—my version of lamb shashliks.

800g (28oz) lamb fillet
6 garlic cloves
¼ fresh kiwi fruit
1 x 375ml (13fl oz) bottle beer (a
   pale ale is good to use)
60ml (2fl oz) Korean chilli paste
2 tablespoons pepper
½ tablespoon salt
1 tablespoon Korean soy sauce
5 bay leaves
1 tablespoon paprika
200ml (7fl oz) olive oil

Cut the lamb into medium-sized cubes.

Mince the garlic and put in a large bowl, then squeeze the juice from the kiwi fruit into the bowl also.

Next add the beer, chilli paste, pepper, salt, soy sauce, bay leaves, paprika and olive oil.

Now add the lamb and marinate in the fridge overnight or for a minimum of 3 hours.

Preheat your charcoal on the barbecue but keep the temperature low. Thread the marinated lamb on shashlik skewers.

Put your prepared lamb shashliks on the barbecue and turn regularly as you don't want them too dry. Barbecue to your taste but I recommend that you don't overcook them.

This goes well with a fresh garden salad.

BBQ Pork Back Ribs
Daeji Galbi

Serves 4

Koreans love to barbecue. I remember many long nights eating a Korean barbecue with family or friends sipping on the Korean drink Soju. The only difference to a Western barbecue is that the Korean barbecue is generally over charcoal in the centre of the table.

1 lemon, juiced
½ cup soju
½ cup water
6 bamboo leaves (available in cryovac, in Asian grocers)
3kg (3lb 10oz) pork back ribs
6 bay leaves
1 tablespoon whole peppercorns
3 tablespoons Korean or Japanese soy sauce
BBQ Dipping Sauce (see recipe in Korean Barbecue at Home)
Olive oil

HOMEMADE BBQ SAUCE
1 brown onion, peeled and quartered
1 small can red plums
2 cups tomato sauce
½ cup white wine vinegar
½ cup mustard sauce
4 tablespoons Worcestershire sauce
2 tablespoons garlic powder
1 cup sugar syrup
1 tablespoon chilli powder
1 splash Tabasco sauce
2 tablespoons thick caramel soy sauce (available from supermarkets and Asian grocers)

Preheat oven to 100°C (210°F). Mix together the lemon juice, soju and water.

On a roasting pan, lay down three bamboo leaves. Next lay the ribs on top, pour over the lemon, soju and water mix, add the bay leaves, whole peppercorns and soy sauce and then place the remaining three bamboo leaves on top.

Cover the tray with foil and cook slowly for 1½ hours.

While the ribs are in the oven, make the barbecue sauce. In a food processor, add the onion and red plums and process into a paste. Add the remaining barbecue sauce ingredients and blend together until well combined. Place in a container and put in the fridge.

Heat the barbecue (preferably a charcoal one).

Remove the ribs from the oven and, before placing on the barbecue, remove the bamboo leaves and dip into the homemade BBQ sauce. Cook for 5 minutes to get that charcoal flavour.

This is a great one to impress your meat-eating friends with.

Korean Barbecue at Home
Samgyupsal Pamuchim

People always associate Korean food with barbecues so here is how you can create your own Korean barbecue at home.

Pork Belly
Samgyupsal

600g (21oz) pork belly
30ml (1fl oz) any white whine
Pinch pepper
Pinch salt
2 bay leaves

Slice the pork belly into long lengths and marinate with remaining ingredients. Refrigerate for at least one hour.

The best way to cook this is either on a charcoal barbecue or Webber.

Simply throw the pork belly on the barbecue and cook through. Enjoy with some of the following sauces.

Dipping Sauce

½ tablespoon salt
Pinch pepper
1 tablespoon sesame oil

In a small bowl, mix everything together.

BBQ Dipping Sauce

¼ brown onion, peeled and
   quartered
¼ apple
½ pineapple, peeled
50g (1¾oz) carrot
2 cloves garlic
2 tablespoons olive oil
1 tablespoon white wine
3 tablespoons vinegar
Splash of Korean soy sauce
1 teaspoon sugar

Put everything in a food processor and combine until it is a
reasonably thick sauce.

Thick Bean Paste
Doenjang Sum Jung

3 tablespoons doenjang sauce
   (bean paste sauce)
2 teaspoons minced garlic
1 tablespoon spring onion
   (scallion), finely diced
1 tablespoon sesame oil
1 teaspoon Korean chilli paste
1 teaspoon sugar
1 teaspoon sesame seeds

Simply mix everything together until well combined.

Note: This barbecue is great to eat with the Leek Salad (see recipe).

sides

Steamed Egg With Shrimp
Kerun Jim

This is my childhood favourite. This dish would often be made after we bought the eggs fresh from the salesmen walking around the street.

2¼ cups water
5 x 10cm (2 x 4in) piece thick
    seaweed (dashima)
6 fresh prawns (shrimp), shelled
    (reserve the shells)
6 eggs
100ml (3½fl oz) milk
Pinch salt
¼ red onion, diced
30g (1oz) carrot, diced
30g (1oz) spring onion (scallion),
    diced

In a saucepan boil 1¼ cups water, seaweed and prawn shells and heads and simmer for 10 minutes to make a stock. In a bowl, whisk the eggs. Sieve the eggs into another bowl and add the milk, salt, vegetables and stock.

Pour the mixture evenly into 3 heatproof ramekins, place two prawns into each ramekin and cover them tightly with aluminium foil.

In a large, wide saucepan, boil 1 cup of water, reduce to a low heat and place the ramekins in the saucepan carefully not allowing any water to get in. Put the saucepan lid on and steam for 15–20 minutes. You will know when this is ready by shaking the ramekins and if the liquid doesn't move it is good to eat.

Steamed Rice

I have a rice cooker, which makes life easier, but cooking rice to perfection on the stove needs a bit more love and care.

2½ cups short-grain white rice
Water

Wash the rice in a bowl until the water becomes clear. Keep 3 cups of water from the last rinse in a separate bowl. Now leave the washed rice to soak in fresh water for 30 minutes to give it more flavour.

In a saucepan, add the drained washed rice and the 3 cups of water from the final rinse and boil for 4 minutes.

Reduce the heat to medium and simmer for three minutes. When the rice starts to look puffed, reduce to a low heat and simmer for another 10 minutes and it is now ready. Do not stir until the end of cooking.

Sides

Leek Salad
Pamuchim

Serves 4

5 leeks
10 spring onions (scallions)
2 tablespoons Korean chilli
   powder
2 tablespoons sugar
2 tablespoons vinegar
1 tablespoon Korean chilli paste
1 tablespoon sesame oil
1 tablespoon sesame seeds
Pinch salt

Slice the leeks extremely finely, about 7–10cm (2¾ x 4in) in length, and put in cold water for 30 minutes.

Drain the leek thoroughly and dry with a towel. Slice the spring onions.

In a separate bowl, mix together by hand the chilli powder, sugar, vinegar, chilli paste, sesame oil, sesame seeds and salt and then mix this together with the leek and spring onions.

Smoked Salmon Rolls

This is another fancy little option for canapés or just a healthy snack.

SALSA
½ brown onion, peeled
½ avocado
1 tablespoon lemon juice
Pinch sugar
Pinch salt

1 cucumber
1 pkt smoked salmon
French Dressing (see recipe)

To make the salsa, finely dice the onion and avocado, then mix together with the lemon juice, sugar and salt.

Using a vegetable peeler, carefully peel the cucumber lengthways into very thin strips.

Lay one piece of salmon down flat. Place a cucumber strip on top and roll carefully.

Repeat to make as many rolls as possible.

To serve, stand up on a plate and put a teaspoon of salsa down the middle of each roll. If you want, you can wrap some extra ribbons of cucumber around the base of the salmon rolls for decoration. Serve with the french dressing.

Bean Sprouts

This is used in a lot of dishes, including rice and noodles.

3 cups bean sprouts
1 tablespoon Korean beef stock
½ teaspoon minced garlic
2 teaspoons sesame oil
½ tablespoon sesame seeds
Pinch salt

Put some water in a saucepan and once it boils, add the bean sprouts and cook for about 2 minutes.

Rinse and drain the bean sprouts. Put bean sprouts in a bowl and toss through the rest of the ingredients.

Spinach
Sigeumchi-namul

1 bunch English spinach
½ teaspoon salt
1 tablespoon Korean beef stock
½ teaspoon minced garlic
2 teaspoons sesame oil
½ tablespoon sesame seeds

Cut the roots off the spinach while boiling some water in a large pan on the stove. Once it boils, blanch the spinach with a big pinch of salt for 2 minutes. Be sure to maintain the green colour.

Take off the heat and rinse thoroughly, then drain by squeezing with your hands. Cut into lengths of 5–6cm (2–2⅓in) long.

Now place squeezed spinach into a mixing bowl, add the remaining ingredients and mix well.

Kimchi

Kimchi is my favourite and a favourite throughout Korea and Japan. If anyone knows anything about Korean food it would be kimchi. So popular is it in Korea that there are kimchi museums and kimchi fridges.

Before refrigeration, Koreans would make enough kimchi in summer to last throughout our very cold winters and it would be buried underground in pots. But now, the leading refrigerator brands have created the kimchi fridge—one of the most wanted household appliances in Korea!

Kimchi is also a healthy and tasty side dish and Koreans believe it even protects against viruses, as there is a fair dose of garlic included.

1 Chinese cabbage
70g (2½oz) cooking salt

MARINADE
1 onion, peeled
20g (²/₃oz) sugar
50g (1¾oz) sugar syrup
1 teaspoon minced ginger
80g (2½oz) Korean chilli powder
200g (7oz) minced garlic
20g (²/₃oz) fish sauce
40g (1½oz) garlic chives

Cut the core out of the cabbage and separate the leaves. Cut each leaf in half longways and then cut into 3½cm (1⅓in) lengths and place in a large bowl. Mix the salt into the cabbage thoroughly with your hands.

Leave the cabbage soaking in the salt for about 2–3 hours.

When the cabbage is floppy, thoroughly wash with water and leave to drain.

To prepare the marinade, blitz the onion in a food processor till it resembles a paste and mix in a large bowl with suguar, sugar syrup, minced ginger, chilli powder, minced garlic and fish sauce. Wash and cut the garlic chives into lengths of 1cm (⅓in). With gloves on, thoroughly mix through with your hands.

Combine the marinade with the cabbage and give a big and thorough mix until cabbage is red.

Put the kimchi in an airtight container and keep in the fridge. It will last for at least one month.

Kimchi is best eaten as a side dish with rice and a main meal or other side dishes. My brother-in-law has been known to eat it on toast, but this is not my recommendation.

Gokdugi

This is another version of kimchi but with radish instead of cabbage. It is best eaten with clear Korean soups. We say the best way to choose the cabbage is to look for one that's short and stumpy like Korean girls' legs (I might get in trouble for saying this!).

1 x 1kg (2lb 4oz) Chinese radish (the thick and stumpy ones are tastier)
25g (¾oz) cooking salt
30g (1oz) Korean chilli powder
50g (1¾oz) minced garlic
25g (¾oz) fish sauce
30g (1oz) sugar

Peel the radish and then chop into pieces approximately 1½ x 1½cm (½ x ½in).

Put the cut radish into a bowl and mix the salt through.

Leave for about 1½ hours until the salt has absorbed and the radish is soft. Then wash the salt off and drain.

While draining, combine the chilli powder, garlic, fish sauce and sugar together, then when ready mix with the cabbage and store in an airtight container.

Leave it out for about 5 hours, then put it in the fridge. This will keep for two weeks if kept in the fridge.

Enjoy with rice—this is a healthy radish dish and is a very traditional Korean side dish.

Tasty Potatoes

This one keeps in the fridge for a couple of days but in my house it is gone in one sitting.

60ml (2fl oz) olive oil
10 medium-sized potatoes,
  peeled and cut into small
  cubes
50ml (1¾fl oz) Korean or Japanese
  soy sauce
120ml sugar syrup or corn syrup
50ml (1¾fl oz) water
Pinch salt
Pinch pepper
1 teaspoon sesame oil
Pinch toasted sesame seeds

Heat the oil in a large frypan and add the potatoes. Toss gently keeping on high and when the potatoes are well coated in oil, slowly add the soy sauce, sugar syrup and water and keep on a high heat for approximately 5 minutes, watching and tossing occasionally. Add the salt and pepper, sesame oil and seeds when the potatoes are just tender.

Try not to touch the potatoes during the cooking process as we do not want to ruin their shape.

Eggplant
Kaji Muchim

An old saying in Korea is that anything purple is good for the health of your body, so this dish is a great one for all you healthy eaters as a side dish or salad.

2 eggplants (aubergine)
½ tablespoon salt
1 tablespoon sugar
1½ tablespoons Korean or
  Japanese soy sauce
3 tablespoons sesame oil
1½ tablespoons minced garlic
2 tablespoons oil
1 bunch spring onions (scallions)
2 tablespoons toasted sesame
  seeds

When choosing the correct eggplant, look for a very firm one with a good purple colour.

Wash the eggplants, slice into 7 x 1cm (2¾ x ⅓in) lengths and sprinkle with salt and sugar. Leave for about 20 minutes or until the eggplant is soft, then squeeze all the juice out.

While the eggplants are soaking, mix together the soy sauce, sesame oil and garlic.

In a frypan, add the oil and reduce to a low heat then add the eggplants and lightly fry them. Add 2 tablespoons water and simmer for 5 minutes. Add the prepared sauce, place a lid on the frypan and simmer for a further 5 minutes.

Slice the spring onions into ½cm (⅛in) lengths and toss in for the last one minute of simmering.

Remove from the heat and serve how you wish, mixing with the toasted sesame seeds.

Bulgogi Salad

This is a popular dish in Mapo for summer. It is my twist on the famous Korean bulgogi and is delicious on sandwiches or wraps for lunch.

300g (10½oz) sirloin beef
½ nashi pear
2 tablespoons Korean or
   Japanese soy sauce
½ tablespoon minced garlic
2 tablespoons sugar syrup
1 tablespoon sesame oil
1 tablespoon soju or sake or
   sweet white wine
Pinch pepper
200g (7oz) lettuce mix
½ container alfalfa sprouts
½ red onion
2 tablespoons oil
100g (3½oz) spring onion (scallion),
   thinly sliced

DRESSING
1 tablespoon toasted sesame
   seeds
4 tablespoons Korean or
   Japanese soy sauce
1 tablespoon white vinegar
1 tablespoon honey
1 tablespoon sesame oil
2 tablespoons olive oil
2 tablespoons fresh lemon juice
2 tablespoons sugar

Slice the beef into thin strips and wrap in a tea towel to remove all excess juices, then place in a mixing bowl. Grate the nashi pear and place in another bowl with the soy sauce, garlic, sugar syrup, sesame oil, soju and pepper and mix thoroughly by hand, then pour over the meat and give a little mix by hand ensuring all the beef is coated. Leave to marinate for 30 minutes.

While the beef is marinating, wash the lettuce and the sprouts and drain, then slice the onion thinly and also wash and drain.

To make the dressing, crush the sesame seeds and then mix all the ingredients together thoroughly.

In a frypan, heat the oil on a very high heat and then add the marinated beef. Flame toss the beef keeping the heat at its highest. When the beef is almost cooked, throw in the spring onion.

Presenting this dish to look its very best is easy. On four plates, evenly place the lettuce, sprouts and onion, then drizzle with the dressing and on top place even amounts of the beef in the centre, creating a restaurant meal at home.

Sushi Omelette

Easy to eat for breakfast, canapés or snack.

10 eggs
3 tablespoons milk
40g (1½oz) plain (all-purpose)
  flour
10g (⅓oz) minced garlic
Pinch salt
Pinch pepper
3 tablespoons water
¼ carrot
50g (1¾oz) Cheddar cheese
100g (3½oz) leg ham
100g (3½oz) Spinach (see recipe)

Preheat the oven to 190°C (375°F).

In a bowl, add 6 eggs and 4 egg whites and whisk together, slowly adding in the milk, flour, garlic, salt, pepper and water. Whisk for about 4 minutes until a skin forms on top and then carefully remove the skin.

Grate the carrot and cheese. Finely dice the ham.

Line a rectangular baking dish with baking paper and pour in the egg mixture. Top one half top with the English spinach and the other half with the carrot. Sprinkle the ham and cheese over both halves and bake for 12 minutes.

Remove from the oven and, while still warm, use a sushi mat to roll the omelette firm, then allow to cool while still in the sushi mat.

Cut evenly into slices and it is now ready to eat.

Oven-baked Garlic

Serves 6

This tastes amazing but it's not good if you're planning on going out after!

6 garlic bulbs
½ cup oil
Pinch salt
Pinch pepper
2 saffron threads

Preheat the oven to low. Each oven varies but between 80–120°C (175–250°F).

Carefully cut the top off each garlic bulb leaving all the skin on. Then in an oven tray place the oil and put in the garlic bulbs. Sprinkle with salt and pepper and the saffron threads.

Cook slowly in the oven for one hour.

This is great with a roast or any Korean dish.

Korean Pickled Vegetables

This can be used with cucumber, onion, bell peppers, radish or any vegetable you like. Use the equivalent of 2 cucumbers or 2 bell peppers or 2 onions.

1½ cups water
1½ cups vinegar
¼ cup salt
2 bay leaves
1 cinnamon stick
½ tablespoon clove
½ tablespoon whole pepper

For the pickling liquid, boil all ingredients together and turn off as soon as it is bubbling, then put into the fridge to cool.

Slice whatever vegetables you choose and put them into a sterilised jar, then pour over the pickling liquid and keep in the fridge for three days.

After three days, drain away the pickling liquid and make a fresh batch of liquid. Put this in a jar with your vegetables and leave in the fridge for another four days. It is then ready to eat.

Lotus Root

When I was growing up I thought only rich people ate this dish. I was told that the long skinny lotus root was the male and the short chunky one was the female. When I buy a lotus root I always choose the 'female'.

400g (14oz) fresh lotus root
50ml (1¾fl oz) oil
2 cups water
3 tablespoons soy sauce (see below)
2 tablespoons sesame oil
1 tablespoon sesame seeds

SOY SAUCE
2 tablespoons Korean soy sauce
1 tablespoon sugar
1 tablespoon mirin
½ tablespoon sugar syrup

Peel the lotus root and thinly slice.

Put the oil in a frypan and heat to medium. Add the lotus pieces with the water and soy sauce ingredients.

Simmer until the sauce has reduced and the colour is a light to medium brown.

Turn off the heat and then quickly mix in the sesame oil and sesame seeds.

Mango, Tomato and Tofu Salad

Mangoes are expensive in Korea so I go wild eating them here in summer. I have created this special salad to eat with my barbecue steak.

1 tablespoon olive oil
8 cherry tomatoes, washed
Pinch pepper
Pinch salt
1 large mango
1 pkt silken tofu
5 mint leaves
10g (¹/₃oz) coriander

SALAD DRESSING
70ml (2½fl oz) balsamic vinegar
30ml (1fl oz) mango puree
10ml (¹/₃fl oz) olive oil
Pinch pepper
Pinch salt

Heat the olive oil in a frypan over a low heat, add the tomatoes and toss slowly. Sprinkle with pepper and salt and continue tossing on a low heat for 5 minutes. Set aside.

Peel the mango and scoop out as many balls as possible with a melon ball scoop. Do the same with the silken tofu.

Wash the mint leaves and coriander.

In a bowl, mix together all the dressing ingredients.

On a flat salad bowl, carefully place the tomatoes, mango balls and tofu balls, forming a coloured pattern of your choice.

Decorate with the mint leaves and coriander and pour over the salad dressing.

Creamy Basil Sweet Soy Sauce Mushrooms

This makes a great accompaniment for any meal.

1 tablespoon butter
400g (14oz) Swiss brown
   mushrooms
1 ladle Creamy Basil Sauce (see
   recipe)
3 tablespoons Ginger-flavoured
   Sweet Soy Sauce (see recipe)

Heat the butter in the frypan and add the whole mushrooms until they are coated in butter and almost cooked. Then add the creamy basil sauce and the ginger-flavoured sweet soy sauce. Once boiling reduce the heat until the sauce is caramelised and sticky.

soups
(jigaes)

Kimchi Stew
Kimchi Jigae

This is a soup that my dad has every morning for breakfast. My mother loves it when she comes to visit me as she gets times off from the daily routine. This dish has lots of vitamin B—I guess it's Koreans equivalent to marmite or vegemite.

8 cups water
100g (3½oz) Chinese radish (daikon), sliced
1 onion, sliced
30g (1oz) thick seaweed (kelp)
1 tablespoon sesame oil
300g (10½oz) kimchi and juice (the older the better for jigae)
1½ tablespoons Korean chilli powder
1 tablespoon garlic
½ tablespoon ginger
Pinch pepper
Pinch salt
150g (5oz) firm tofu, cubed
Spring onions (scallions), finely sliced

Make stock by boiling 8 cups water and adding Chinese radish, onion and seaweed. Boil for 30 minutes or until radish is soft.

In a saucepan, add the sesame oil and fry the kimchi lightly for a couple of minutes. Add chilli powder, garlic, ginger, pepper and salt, and continue to fry at a low temperature. Now add 4 cups of the radish and onion stock, then add some of the kimchi juice and bring to the boil. When boiling, reduce the heat and simmer for about 30 minutes. Just before you are ready to eat, add the cubed tofu and sliced spring onions. You may need to add more stock during cooking as it may evaporate.

Serve with a bowl of rice, and if you like it really spicy add some fresh chilli. This soup can be eaten as vegetarian or you can add tuna or pork belly.

Cockle Soup

Every year we go cockling and this is what I make with the cockles my children collect for me.

350g (12oz) cockles
5 cups cold water
2 tablespoons salt
5 cups water
2 cloves garlic
10g (⅓oz) fresh ginger, thinly sliced
2 teaspoons sea salt
Pinch pepper
1 tablespoon white wine
1 sprig spring onion (scallion),
  chopped
1 red chilli, chopped
1 green chilli, chopped
10g (⅓oz) chrysanthemum leaves

Put the cockles in the cold water with the salt and leave for half a day, covered. This will encourage the cockles to spit out all the sand and be clean.

Once the cockles are ready, rinse thoroughly. Boil 5 cups of water and add the cockles. Cook on a high heat until they are open. Remove immediately.

With a sieve, scoop out all the waste from the stock. Reheat the stock, add the garlic and ginger and boil for 5 minutes. Add the sea salt, pepper, white wine, spring onion and chillies. Once boiling again, take off the heat.

Finely dice the chrysanthemum leaves.

In two bowls evenly pour the stock, then add the cockles and garnish with the chrysanthemum leaves.

Large Kimchi Soup To Share
Budae Kimchi Jungol

This large soup was created by the army using leftover tins of spam and kimchi and whatever else they could find. Don't screw your nose up at the thought of spam—this actually tastes delicious. Here's my version!

2 tablespoons Korean chilli paste
1 tablespoon minced garlic
1 tablespoon Korean soy sauce
1 tablespoon mirin
Pinch Korean curry powder
1 Vienna sausage or frankfurter
1 tin spam
5 rashers middle bacon
2 spring onions (scallions)
300g (10½oz) firm tofu
2 red chilli
1 brown onion, peeled and sliced
200g (7oz) baked beans
2 mild cheese slices
100g (3½oz) cabbage, sliced
½ cup kimchi
140g (5oz) plain ramen noodles
400ml (14fl oz) beef stock, made
  with 1 tablespoon Korean beef
  stock and 400ml (14fl oz) water

In a small bowl, combine the chilli paste, minced garlic, soy sauce, mirin and curry powder by hand with gloves on. Form the paste into a ball.

Slice the Vienna sausage into pieces about 0.3cm (⅛in) thick.

Cut the spam into slices of 0.3 cm (⅛in) thick and then cut in half.

Cut the bacon into pieces a similar size to the spam.

Wash the spring onions and then slice julienne-style into pieces the same size as the sausage.

Cut the tofu into cubes about 3 x 3 cm (1¼ x 1¼in).

Wash and cut the chilli into slices.

Now either in a jungol pan (similar to a paella pan) or a large frypan, place the chilli paste ball, Vienna sausages, spam, bacon, brown onion, spring onions, tofu, chilli, baked beans, cheese, cabbage and kimchi in separate mounds, filling up the pan, but do not add the noodles yet.

Pour the beef stock over the ingredients and bring to the boil, then add the noodles, continuing to boil until the noodles are cooked. This dish is best eaten with a side of rice.

The best way to eat and cook this is by using a portable gas cooker. That way, while you are sitting at the table talking, your tasty soup is simmering away in front of you.

Ginseng Chicken Soup
Samgetang

This is known as stamina food to beat the long humid months of summer in Korea. It is a healthy version of chicken soup, introducing Korean's favourite—ginseng root.

2 extra small chickens
½ cup sticky rice
1 cup water
4 Korean ginseng roots
4 dried dates
20 cloves garlic
2 bunches spring onion (scallions)
4 fresh chestnuts
2 litres (70fl oz) water
Pepper and salt

Wash the chickens thoroughly and leave to drain. Put the sticky rice in 1 cup of cold water until the water turns white, which should take about 30 minutes. While the rice is soaking, peel the ginseng skin and cut off the root, and remove the stones from the dates.

Peel the garlic and slice the washed spring onions into small 1cm (¼in) lengths.

With a tablespoon, stuff the prepared rice into the chickens in equal amounts.

On one of the chickens legs, make a small cut just big enough to fit the other leg. Now cross the other leg and slip it into the cut so it is secure. Repeat with the second chicken.

In a large saucepan, place 2 litres of cold water and add the chickens, ginseng roots, dates, chestnuts and garlic and bring to the boil. On a high heat, boil rapidly for 30 minutes and then simmer on a low heat for a further 30 minutes. Remove the chickens and carefully pour the stock into another bowl or saucepan through a fine sieve or cloth to remove excess oil.

Now reboil the stock and add the spring onions, a pinch of pepper and salt, along with the chicken. It is now ready to eat straightaway.

To serve, place the chickens into two large serving bowls and pour over the stock and all ingredients. The way to eat this is for two people to share one bowl each.

Soft Tofu Soup
Sundubu

150g (5oz) kimchi (the older the
  better)
1 brown onion
1 stem spring onion (scallion)
1 tablespoon oil
1 tablespoon minced garlic
1 teaspoon sesame oil
2½ cups vegetable stock
1 tablespoon Korean chilli
  powder
1 pkt (180g/6oz) silken tofu
Pinch salt
1 egg

If you have a clay pot this is best; if not, just use a saucepan.

Dice the kimchi and onion finely. Thinly slice the spring onion into circles.

Heat the oil, add the diced kimchi and onion and fry with the minced garlic and sesame oil until the onion is golden brown. Add the vegetable stock and chilli powder, bring to the boil, then simmer for 20 minutes. If the stock is reduced a lot add a little water.

Just before you are ready to remove from the heat, add the silken tofu, spring onion, salt and egg.

This is best served with a freshly cooked bowl of steamed rice.

Black Shell Mussel Soup

Serves 2 (big eaters)

This is a simple but tasty clear soup.

300g (10½oz) Chinese radish (daikon)
1 thick sheet seaweed (dashima)
1 litre (36fl oz) water
1 tablespoon soy sauce
1 tablespoon Korean beef stock
2 tablespoons oil
1 tablespoon minced garlic
1kg (2lb 4oz) black shell mussels
½ tablespoon salt
Pinch pepper
3 spring onions (scallions), washed and finely sliced

Cut the radish into about 4 pieces and break the seaweed up into 6 pieces. Boil the water in a large pot and add the Chinese radish, soy sauce, beef stock and thick seaweed. Continuing boiling for 20 minutes.

In a frypan, add the oil and fry the minced garlic and cleaned black shell mussels, adding salt and pepper. This should only take about 2 minutes, then add to the stock and boil for a further 10 minutes or until the mussels have opened.

Turn off the heat. It is best to remove the mussels that have opened and, preferably, leave the unopened mussels in the stock until they open.

To serve, divide the stock up into bowls and add the mussels topped with spring onions.

desserts

Green Tea Bread Loaves

This is great variation on your traditional white bread loaf.

130g (4½oz) strong flour (bread flour)
120g (4oz) plain (all-purpose) flour
10g (⅓oz) sugar
½ teaspoon salt
½ teaspoon instant dry yeast
10g (⅓oz) green tea (matcha) powder
90–95ml (3fl oz) warm water
1 egg
10g (⅓oz) butter, softened
Oil
Flour, for dusting

These toppings are great to make a sandwich with your fresh green tea loaf:

Alfafa
Tomato
Cheese
Ham
Mayonnaise
Mustard
Onion
Gherkin

Sift the strong flour and plain flour into a large bowl.

Now divide the flour evenly into three mounds on a flat surface. Add the sugar to one mound, the salt to another and the yeast powder to another and then mix each mound with your hands. When well combined mix all three mounds together.

Add the green tea powder, warm water, egg and softened butter and knead, making sure the butter is mixed in thoroughly. It should now have a shiny green appearance.

Wrap and leave in a warm area of your house for 40–50 minutes. It should almost double in size.

Knead well to get rid of any air bubbles and then divide the mix into three oblong shapes.

Put an oven tray cover with a warm damp cloth and leave in a warm area for a further 45 minutes.

Preheat the oven to 200°C (400°F). Spray the loaves lightly with oil and then sprinkle with a layer of plain flour. With a sharp knife make two cuts in each loaf longways on the top.

Bake for 20 minutes.

This loaf is delicious eaten straight out of the oven or when cooled. Slice to serve.

Coconut Crème Brûlée

This is my Asian twist on the famous French dessert.

400ml (14fl oz) coconut milk
   (1 can)
360g (12oz) egg yolk
210g (7oz) sugar
300ml (10½fl oz) full cream milk
900ml (32fl oz) thickened cream
   (light whipping cream)

Preheat the oven to 160°C (320°F).

In a saucepan, add enough water so it is about 4cm (1½in) up the side, then on a low heat place the opened tin of coconut milk into the saucepan and gently heat until it is warm.

In a separate bowl whisk together the egg yolk and sugar. When the coconut milk is ready, add this and give it a good whisk. Then add the milk and cream and mix thoroughly.

Pour the mixture gently into another bowl while sieving it through and then repeat this process twice.

Pour the mixture into ramekins leaving about 1cm (⅓in) the top. In a baking dish, put some water and carefully place the ramekin pots in, not allowing any water to enter the pots.

Cook in the oven for 45 minutes, you will know when they are ready as the centre is slightly wobbly.

Set aside to cool down, still in the hot water.

When you are ready to serve the crème brûlée, sprinkle 2 teaspoons of sugar across the top, spreading evenly. Use a domestic blowtorch to torch the sugar on top until it becomes golden brown and caramelised in the form of toffee.

If you don't have a blowtorch you can achieve the same effect by placing the crème brûlées under a grill.

Deep-fried Honey Cookies
Yakgwa

This is the most luxurious and tasteful Korean cookie, served on festival days during ceremonial feasts and at memorial services.

1 cup wheat flour (medium
   viscidness)
2 tablespoons sesame oil
4 cups vegetable oil
sliced pine nuts, for decoration
   (optional)

SEASONING
2 tablespoons honey
2 tablespoons refined rice wine
Pinch salt
Pinch white pepper
Pinch cinnamon powder
½ tablespoon ginger juice

HONEY SYRUP
1 cup honey
Pinch cinnamon powder

Sieve the wheat flour into a bowl and mix with the sesame oil, then sieve again.

Add all the seasoning ingredients, mix thoroughly and then knead it softly. Roll the dough flat and fold as many times as needed to make it about ½cm (⅛in) thick.

Cut into 3.5cm (1⅓in) squares and make about 6 holes in each biscuit with a chopstick.

Blend the honey syrup.

Pour the oil into a large pan or wok and heat it to medium heat (about 5 minutes). When the oil is ready, put in the prepared cookies and fry for 15 minutes.

When the cookies begin to float on the surface, raise the heat and fry for another 10 minutes until both sides turn honey brown.

Using a strainer, drain the biscuits of the oil and leave to stand for 10 minutes.

Place the biscuits in the honey syrup for 5–6 hours and then drain using a strainer again for an hour. You may use sliced pine nuts on top for a garnish.

Sweet Pancake
Hoddeok

This is a very popular street food dessert. It is served between a small piece of folded cardboard and is really hot and tasty. Enjoy Korea's version of a sweet pancake.

DOUGH
200ml (7fl oz) milk
120g (4oz) margarine
2kg (4lb 6oz) plain (all-purpose) flour
100g (3½oz) sticky rice flour
35g (1¼oz) sugar
12g (½oz) salt
2 teaspoons dried yeast
25g (¾oz) corn flour (corn starch)
¾ teaspoon vanilla essence
3 eggs

FILLING
1.5 kg (3lb 5oz) plain (all-purpose) flour
400g (14oz) crushed peanuts
150g (5oz) crushed pumpkin seeds
150g (5oz) crushed sunflower seeds
100g (3½oz) cinnamon powder
750g (1lb 10oz) dark brown sugar

Oil for cooking, approximately 50ml (1¾fl oz)

In a saucepan, warm the milk and add the margarine until fully dissolved and warm. In a mixing bowl, sift together the plain flour and sticky rice flour and slowly mix in the milk and margarine mixture by hand to make the dough.

Divide the dough evenly into three mounds on a flat surface. Add the sugar to one mound, the salt to another and the yeast powder to another and mix each mound with your hands, then when well combined mix all three mounds together.

Add the corn flour, vanilla essence and eggs and mix thoroughly to complete the dough. Wrap in plastic wrap, leaving some breathing holes, and sit in a warm place until the dough has risen.

To make the filling, finely grind all the ingredients together.

When the dough is ready, measure out about 60g (2oz) for each hoddeok and, holding in one hand, make a well in the mixture and add one tablespoon of the filling. Close over so it is now a ball shape and repeat this for all hoddeoks.

In a small frypan, heat some oil. When hot add one hoddeok and press down to make your pancake, then cook on a low heat, turning a few times until cooked through and golden brown.

Sweet Potato Cake

Serves 6

This is our version of sweet cake. Koreans love it as we think it is still healthy as it is made from a vitamin-filled vegetable.

3 eggs
90g (3oz) sugar
90g (3oz) plain flour
30g (1oz) butter
1½ teaspoons vanilla essence
¼ teaspoon baking powder

FILLING
800g–1kg (28oz–2lb 4oz) sweet
    potato
60g (2oz) butter
100g (3½oz) sugar
200ml (7fl oz) milk
200ml (7fl oz) thickened cream
    (light whipping cream)

TOPPING
2 tablespoons sugar
200g (7oz) thickened cream (light
    whipping cream)
pecans, for decoration (optional)

Preheat the oven to 180°C (350°F).

To make the sponge, beat eggs and slowly add the sugar until the mixture becomes stiffened. Then add all remaining cake ingredients and beat until well combined. Pour the mixture into a greased 20cm (8in) round cake tin and bake for about 25 minutes or until cooked through.

Set aside on a wire rack to cool.

To make the filling, peel and cut the sweet potato into smallish pieces and boil until soft, usually only about 15 minutes. Drain then mash the potato but not too well as it is best to have it quite thick. Set aside to cool.

In a saucepan, add the butter, sugar, milk and cream and boil, mixing all the time. Take off the heat and let cool for 10 minutes, then bring to the boil again and let it cool. When you have heated the mixture two times, add to the mashed sweet potato, mixing thoroughly.

The topping can be prepared now by beating the sugar and cream together until thick.

When the cake has cooled, very carefully with a sharp knife slice it evenly into three. Now it is time to assemble the cake.

Put the bottom piece of cake on a plate and spread half of the filling mixture onto the top, then add the middle piece of cake and spread the remaining filling onto the top of that. Finally add the top piece and spread the topping onto the top of the cake.

You can decorate the top with sliced pecans to add a special finish to the sweet potato cake.

Twist Donuts

Every year when we would cater at the McLaren Vale Sea and Vines food and wine festival this would be our specialty dessert. We would sell out each day, leaving the punters wanting more for the next day. Let's see if you can stop at just one!

440g (15oz) strong flour (bread flour)

110g (3½oz) plain (all-purpose) flour

55g (2oz) sugar

1½ teaspoons salt

2 packets (½oz) dried yeast powder

2 eggs

16g (½oz) coffee mate

240ml (8½fl oz) warm water

66g (2oz) unsalted butter, softened

½ teaspoon vanilla essence

Oil for frying

½ cup sugar, for rolling the cooked donuts in

Sift the strong flour and plain flour into a large bowl. Divide the flour evenly into three mounds on a flat surface. Add the sugar to one mound, the salt to another and the yeast powder to another and then mix each mound with your hands. When well combined mix all three mounds together. Add the eggs and mix well. You may transfer to a bowl if easier, then add the coffee mate and water and combine well.

With your hands, add the softened butter and vanilla essence to make the dough and work in well until it is smooth with no lumps. Continue to knead the dough for about 20 minutes. Cover with cling film and pierce in 6 places allowing the dough to breathe.

Once the mixture has doubled in size, do the 'belly button' check and put your finger in the centre of the dough—if it resembles a navel then it's ready.

Separate the dough into as many 80g (2½oz) balls as you can. Using a rolling pin, roll each ball into a long thin shape about 30–40cm (12–16in) in length. Then fold in half and twist together 4 times.

Lay on baking paper and rest for a further 15 minutes. They should then appear a little fatter.

Heat the oil in a large pan or saucepan on a medium–low heat and when hot, cook the donuts. This should only take a few minutes or until they float to the top. Drain on baking paper and then roll in sugar.

NOTE: When the dough reaches a temperature of 28–30°C (82–86°F) it is the perfect temperature for baking. When you do the 'belly button' test and the dough feels warm, it is the right temperature. Yeast and sugar and salt should not touch each other.

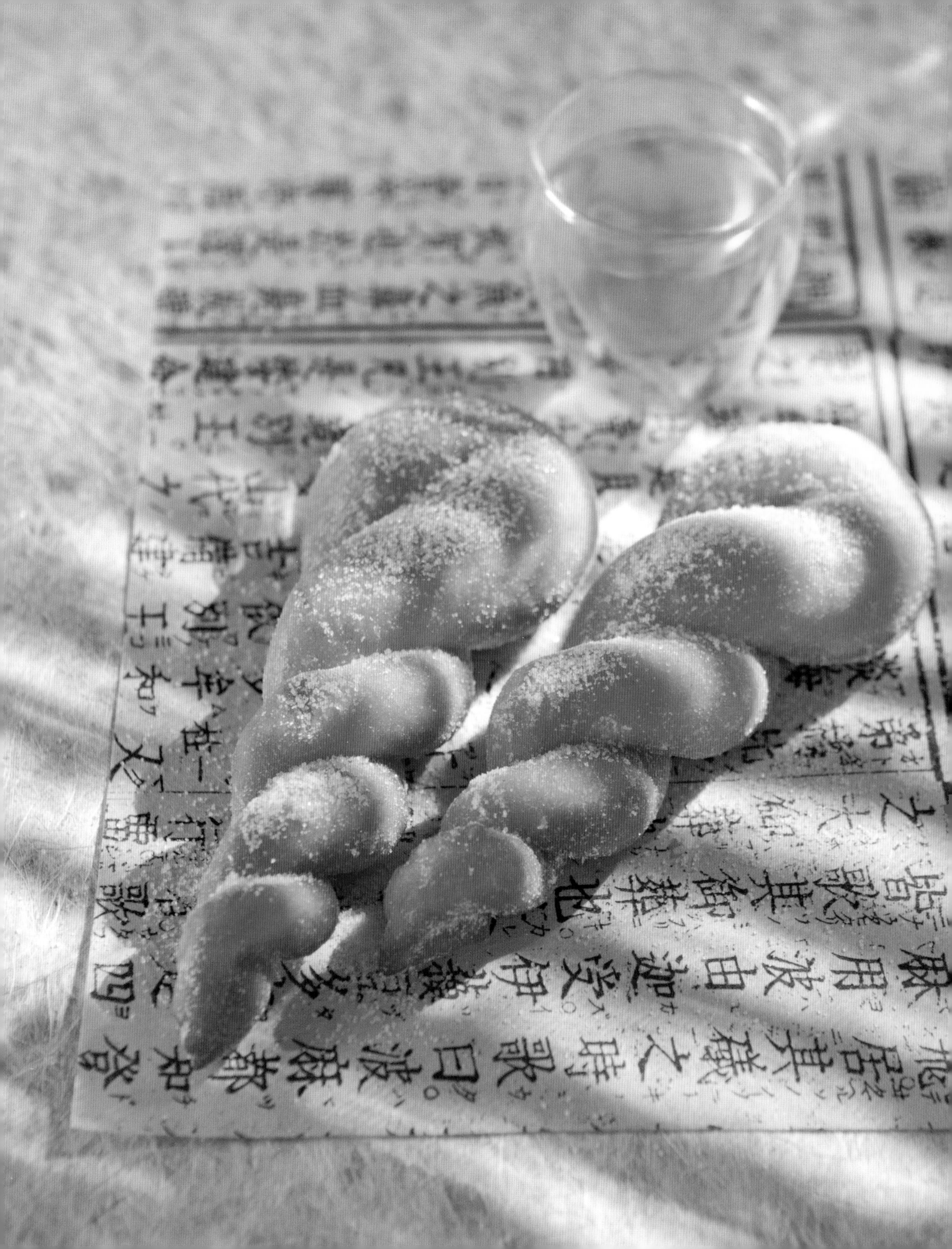

Persimmon Mousse

Persimmon is my favourite fruit ever so I created a dessert I knew I would love.

100g (3½oz) well-ripened
   persimmons
30g (1oz) sugar
1 teaspoon Cointreau
1 sheet gelatine
1 cup cold water
100g (3½oz) thickened cream

SAUCE
100g (3½oz) well-ripened
   persimmons
50ml (1¾fl oz) water
50g (1¾oz) sugar

Use a sieve to push through the well-ripened persimmon so you have a nice clean puree. Mix together with the sugar and Cointreau. Soak the gelatine in cold water until it is soft, then remove and mix with persimmon, sugar and Cointreau using a wooden spoon. Once this is dissolved, whip the cream to a medium texture and add to the mixture.

In small cups of your choice, add the mixture evenly and place in the fridge to set for 2 hours.

To make the sauce, once again sieve the persimmon to form a puree and add the water and sugar .

To serve this mousse, put the cup on a plate and drizzle the sauce around to add some extra flair. This is also great to use as a dipping sauce.

Chocolate Pudding

Makes 12 puddings

This recipe is a little time consuming but worth it and great if you need to make a gluten-free treat.

90g (3oz) unsalted butter
450g (15oz) dark chocolate
150g (5oz) thickened cream
6 eggs, separated
180g (6oz) sugar
80g (2½oz) gluten-free plain flour
40g (1½oz) cocoa powder
1 teaspoon gluten-free baking
 powder
Oil for spraying

TOFFEE GARNISH
100g (3½oz) sugar syrup
100g (3½oz) castor (superfine)
 sugar

CHOCOLATE SAUCE
500g (17½oz) thickened cream
 (light whipping cream)
500g (17½oz) dark chocolate
240g (8½oz) sugar syrup

In a saucepan, heat some water on a low heat. In a heatproof bowl add the butter, dark chocolate and cream and stir occasionally over the water until everything is melted and smooth. Don't let the water touch the bottom of the bowl.

Separate the eggs and through a sieve add the egg yolk to the melted mixture.

Beat the egg whites using a mixer or hand-held beater on high, gradually adding the sugar until it starts to resemble a meringue and appears shiny.

Take out a quarter of the meringue mixture and sift in the gluten-free plain flour, cocoa powder and baking powder until well combined.

Slowly combine the chocolate mix with the quarter of the meringue mixture you removed and when combined add the remaining meringue mixture gently. Put in the fridge for about 1½ hours to rest the gluten mix.

Heat the oven to 220°C (430°F).

In small pudding pots, spray each one with oil and carefully fill the pots two-thirds full with the mixture.

Bake in the oven for 20–30 minutes, or to test shake one of the pots— if the middle is moving it needs a little longer.

Desserts

To make the toffee garnish, boil the sugar syrup and castor sugar together and keep boiling until it becomes golden brown. When ready place the saucepan in cold water. I love to create my own designs with this simply by using a knife or spoon and drizzling the toffee over some baking paper. Get creative and make letters, leaves, music notes, whatever you like. This makes a great decoration on your lovely pudding when serving up to your loved ones.

To make the chocolate sauce bring the cream to the boil. Add the chocolate and once melted, add in the sugar syrup.

To serve this you could put it in a shot glass next to the pudding so each individual can pour it over the pudding themselves. Serve it warm.

This will keep in the fridge so it is also great for heating up and pouring over ice-cream.

sauces

teriyaki sauce

bean paste sauce

honey
mustard
dressing

Korean soy
sauce

tartare
sauce

bokbunja

ginger lime
sauce

gold sauce

sashimi
sauce

Baby Spinach Sauce

The colour of this sauce is impressive to use when decorating your plates and is tasty.

250g (9oz) baby spinach leaves
200ml (7fl oz) olive oil
Pinch salt

Put all the ingredients in a blender and then, when well combined, push through a sieve two times.

Tartare Sauce

My tartare sauce always have our customers asking what I put in it.

1 cup gherkins
1 onion
200g (7oz) Korean mayonnaise
2 tablespoons sugar
4 tablespoons concentrated
   lemon juice
Pinch pepper

Blend the gherkins in a food processor and finely dice the onion. Mix together with the mayonnaise, sugar, lemon juice and a pinch of pepper.

Choo Chee Sauce

This sauce goes great with fish.

50g (1¾oz) palm sugar
40g (1½oz) choo chee paste
270ml (9½fl oz) coconut milk

In a saucepan melt the palm sugar, add the choo chee paste until it is shiny and then pour in the coconut milk. When it is boiling reduce the heat and simmer for 10 minutes.

Walnut Sauce

A tasty salad dressing or great to use as a dipping sauce for almost anything.

100g (3½oz) walnuts
50g (1¾oz) unsalted butter
100ml (3½fl oz) balsamic vinegar
30ml (1fl oz) olive oil

To make the sauce, grind the walnuts and then toss in a medium heat frypan until dark brown. Add the butter and once melted turn off the heat.

In a separate frypan on a medium heat boil the balsamic vinegar, then simmer for 5-10 minutes or until reduced. Turn off the heat. Add the balsamic vinegar and olive oil together in a separate bowl and combine with the walnut mix.

Wild Raspberry Sauce
Bokbunja

I use this as a dipping sauce for any red meat or as a delicious marinade when barbecuing.

½ onion
80g (2½oz) butter
250ml (9fl oz) dry red wine
300ml (10½fl oz) Bokbunja or
   Black Raspberry Wine

Dice the onion finely and fry with the butter until soft. Pour in the dry red wine and bokbunja until boiling, then reduce the heat and simmer for 15 minutes.

Peanut Sauce

This sauce is the best accompaniment for Money Bags.

800g (28oz) peanuts
100ml (3½fl oz) oyster sauce
100ml (3½fl oz) sugar syrup
½ x 400ml (14fl oz) can coconut
   milk
50ml (1¾fl oz) lemon juice
500ml (17½fl oz) Korean
   mayonnaise

Crush the peanuts and mix all the ingredients together.

Cold Roll Peanut Sauce

I learnt this recipe from my Vietnamese sister-in-law. It goes great with rice paper rolls.

4 tablespoons peanut butter
1 tablespoon Korean soy sauce
2 tablespoons hoisin sauce
1 teaspoon Korean chilli sauce
2 tablespoons ground peanuts
1 teaspoon sesame seeds
1 tablespoon lemon juice

Mix all the ingredients together in a bowl.

Ginger Lime Sauce

Best served with our famous Ginger Pork Balls but I also love to use this as a pizza base.

1 red onion
2 fresh chillies
1 tablespoon olive oil
1 tablespoon Korean chilli paste
350ml (12fl oz) sweet chilli sauce
½ cup lime juice

Dice the onion and chillies finely. Heat the oil in a pot, add the chilli paste and stir until smooth. Now add the chilli and onions and fry for about 2 minutes, then add the sweet chilli sauce and lime juice and simmer for 20 minutes, stirring regularly.

Creamy Basil Sauce

This creamy sauce goes well with vegetables or game.

100g (3½oz) fresh Thai basil
2 teaspoons unsalted butter
5 teaspoons sugar
600ml (21fl oz) thickened cream

Chop the basil finely and in a frypan heat the butter. Fry the basil then add the sugar and cream. When boiling reduce the heat and simmer on low for a further 10 minutes.

Chung Jae's GOLD Sauce

Used as the base for a lot of Korean marinades, it can be kept in the fridge for about four weeks.

2 parts soy sauce
2 parts water
1 part sugar

Mix together and boil for 5 minutes. This is good with anything!

Honey Mustard Dressing

This is a great all-rounder for chicken burgers, salad dressing, deep-fried cheese or whatever you choose.

3 tablespoons Korean
  mayonnaise
2 tablespoons honey
1 tablespoon mustard
1 tablespoon lemon juice
4 mint leaves
Pinch pepper
Pinch salt
3 tablespoons minced onion

Whisk all the ingredients together in a bowl.

French Dressing

I like to make this dressing one to go with a nice fresh salad.

½ tablespoon mustard
1 tablespoon concentrated
  lemon juice
4 tablespoons olive oil
4 tablespoons vinegar
1 tablespoon sugar
1 teaspoon salt
3 tablespoons onion juice
1 tablespoon chopped olives
1 tablespoon chopped gherkin
Pinch pepper
1 teaspoon parsley, chopped

Mix all the ingredients together in a bowl.

Thousand Island Dressing

This is great with salad but I always like to add it to sandwiches.

4 tablespoons Korean
   mayonnaise
3 tablespoons tomato sauce
   (ketchup)
1 tablespoons onion, finely
   chopped
1 tablespoon gherkin, finely
   chopped
1 tablespoon gherkin water
1 tablespoon white vinegar
½ tablespoon thickened cream
Pinch pepper

Mix all the ingredients together in a bowl.

Kiwi Fruit Dressing

Great for a summer salad. My mum even puts it over her fruit salad.

1 kiwi fruit, pulped
4 slices tinned pineapple rings,
   blended
¼ cup full cream milk
1 cup olive oil
½ cup white vinegar
3 tablespoons sugar
Pinch salt
Pinch minced garlic

Whisk all the ingredients together in a bowl.

Sashimi Sauce

This is an authentic sauce for any fresh fish. But it can be a little sour.

3 tablespoons Korean chilli paste
2 tablespoons white vinegar
2 tablespoons lemonade
½ tablespoon sugar
Pinch toasted sesame seeds
½ teaspoon minced ginger

Mix all the ingredients together in a bowl.

Bean Paste Sauce

This is great for dipping your cooked BBQ meat in.

2 tablespoons Korean bean paste
1 teaspoon Korean chilli powder
1 teaspoon Korean soy sauce
½ teaspoon sugar
1 tablespoon finely chopped
    spring onion
2 tablespoons minced garlic
1 tablespoon toasted sesame
    seeds
1 tablespoon sesame oil

Mix all the ingredients together in a bowl.

Mustard Sauce

This is great to add to a home-made burger or simply have with your steak.

2 tablespoons horseradish
2 tablespoons orange juice
1 tablespoon sugar
4 tablespoons white vinegar
2 tablespoons sugar syrup
1 tablespoon minced garlic
1 teaspoon salt
Pinch pepper
1 teaspoon sesame oil

Mix all the ingredients together in a bowl.

Ginger-flavoured Sweet Soy Sauce

This is much tastier than store-bought sauce. Works best with beef and chicken.

500ml (17½fl oz) water
4 tablespoons thick seaweed
stock (made from half a sheet of
thick seaweed/dashima)

3 tablespoons Japanese or
   Korean soy sauce
3 tablespoons sugar
3 tablespoons soju or sake
3 tablespoons ginger juice

Boil the water and add half a sheet of thick seaweed to make the stock. Boil soy sauce, sugar, soju, ginger juice and thick seaweed stock until it appears sticky and shiny.

Keeps in the fridge for up to one month.

Index